PRAISE FOR *GET BIG THINGS DONE*

"The opportunity is even bigger than you imagined it. Don't look away, don't blink, this book and this moment are your chance to matter."

—*Seth Godin, author,* What to Do When It's Your Turn

"Good leaders increasingly need to nurture new sources of expertise and ideas beyond what they know . . . to succeed and to be inspired. *Get Big Things Done* is just the guidebook for making the most use of your networks to spark change and meaning."

—*Beth Comstock, Chief Marketing Officer, GE*

"*Get Big Things Done* is a passionate look at a new wave of leaders. It's full of inspiring stories about imaginative ways to forge meaningful connections and achieve audacious goals."

—*Adam Grant, Wharton professor and* New York Times *bestselling author of* Give and Take

"As our interconnectedness grows, so does our collective responsibility to ask the hard questions. *Get Big Things Done* reminds us not only that our action and inaction can have enormous consequences, but that we have the tools we need to tackle the world's biggest problems. It is both an inspiration and provocation to create the world of which we dream. Buy this book for yourself and share with others who want to act now."

—*Jacqueline Novogratz, CEO, Acumen and author of* The Blue Sweater

"Innovation in the Social Era happens when we connect people, ideas and things. *Get Big Things Done* spotlights the power each of us has to generate big value."

—*Nilofer Merchant, author of* 11 Rules for Creating Value in the Social Era

"The essence of creative inspiration is seeing something in a new way. This inspiring book shows us the incredible creative power we have when we connect outside ourselves in meaningful ways. What the authors call Connectional Intelligence will be at the heart of how we as individuals, teams, and companies create—solutions, value, trust, and loyalty—in the twenty-first century."

—*John Seifert, Chairman/CEO, Ogilvy & Mather North America*

"Erica and Saj-nicole get it. We have to connect to create—and the way we connect creates who we are and what we do. With sage observations, keen advice, and great stories, this book gets to the heart of what the authors aptly call 'the power of us.'"

—*Joshua Wolf Shenk, author of* Powers of Two

"We have big things to do in this world and making them happen requires ambition, courage, and above all, each other. *Get Big Things Done* shows the power that is unleashed when we as human beings connect with others. It is an inspirational read that makes you not only want to tackle your biggest, wildest, most ambitious dreams, but shows you how."

—*Maria Eitel, Founding President and CEO, NIKE Foundation*

"*Get Big Things Done* is the rare book that shows us how to understand and harness the tremendous value of today's connected world and how leaders must put this to work in both strategy and execution. It's part map and part inspiration for unlocking the extraordinary potential of our ecosystems and succeeding in our most important endeavors. "

—*Johan Aurik, Managing Partner and Chairman, A.T. Kearney*

"Erica and Saj-nicole have created an important resource for anyone trying to leverage the value of our world's interconnectedness for tangible impact. I am particularly proud that as one of our Global Shapers, Erica is enlisting readers into communities of interests, purpose and finally impact. These are the most core principles of the World Economic Forum."

—*Professor Klaus Schwab, Founder and Executive Chairman, World Economic Forum*

"Understanding the power that comes through connecting and combining each of our talents and gifts with others in this world will be one of our most powerful assets in making the world a better place. *Get Big Things Done* shows us not just the why but the how."

—*Helene Gayle, M.D., M.P.H., President and CEO, CARE*

"The future success of business requires recognizing the changing work landscape. While talent models have evolved over time, approaches that resonate with one segment of the employee population may fall flat with others. *Get Big Things Done* teaches us all how to connect across generations to achieve breakthrough results and grow into the future. Anyone in a leadership position today, or who aspires to be in one in the future, should read this book."

—*Jim Moffatt, Chairman and CEO, Deloitte Consulting LLP*

"Connected-ness is the way forward for women and men that want break-through results. Connectional Intelligence is the how. A must read for anyone with big goals in mind."

—*Sallie Krawcheck, Chairman, Ellevate*

"Not only is *Get Big Things Done* rich in stories and brimming with motivation, it gives a practical framework to help business leaders and entrepreneurs leverage Connectional Intelligence to radically transform their organizations. I'll be referencing this book for a long time."

—*Scott Gerber, CEO, Young Entrepreneur Council*

"Connectional Intelligence is a timely and important concept to understand. In an ever-increasingly interconnected world, the opportunity to integrate knowledge to create innovative solutions has never been greater."

—*Jeff Rosenthal, Co-founder, Summit*

GET
BIG
THINGS DONE

THE POWER OF
CONNECTIONAL
INTELLIGENCE

ERICA DHAWAN AND **SAJ-NICOLE JONI**

St. Martin's Press
New York

GET BIG THINGS DONE. Copyright © 2015 by Erica Dhawan and Saj-nicole Joni. All rights reserved. Printed in the United States of America. For information, address St. Martin's Press, 175 Fifth Avenue, New York, N.Y. 10010.

www.stmartins.com

Designed by Letra Libre

Library of Congress Cataloging-in-Publication Data

Dhawan, Erica.
   Get big things done : the power of connectional intelligence / Erica Dhawan and Saj-nicole Joni.
      p.   cm.
   ISBN 978-1-137-27978-1 (hardcover)
   1. Information technology—Economic aspects. 2. Information technology—Social aspects. 3. Technological innovations. 4. Problem solving. 5. Information society. 6. Online social networks. I. Joni, Saj-nicole A. II. Title.
   HC79.I55D52   2015
   303.48'33—dc23

                                                            2014033944

Our books may be purchased in bulk for promotional, educational, or business use. Please contact your local bookseller or the Macmillan Corporate and Premium Sales Department at 1-800-221-7945, extension 5442, or by e-mail at MacmillanSpecialMarkets@macmillan.com.

First published by Palgrave Macmillan, a division of St. Martin's Press LLC

First Edition: February 2015

10   9   8   7   6

CONTENTS

*To Tess and Kathy for their joy, love,
laughter, and support —SNJ*

*To Rahul, my husband, for his endless love,
encouragement, and belief in my fullest potential —ED*

PART 1

1

THE BIG WAVE

THEY CALL THEM SIMPLY "BIG WAVES." BUT THE PHRASE seems hardly adequate to describe the towering avalanches of water that can rise between sixty and one hundred feet above sea level. If you've never seen such a wave, it can be hard to comprehend just how big it is. Imagine six cars piled bumper to bumper, vertically, into the sky. A wave as tall as a small office building, as long as the distance between first base and third base on a baseball diamond. These monster waves don't look like normal waves, and they don't behave like them either. They reach their incredible size by gathering strength from neighboring waves, absorbing three or four into one massive swell. Their energy is almost kinetic; their movements are impossible to predict.

We believe that connectional intelligence is, metaphorically speaking, the monster wave of our time. Since the turn of the twentieth century, people have dreamt of a world in which technology will enable men and women to create things with their minds, just as machines transformed the means of production in the Industrial Age.

In 1945, Dr. Vannevar Bush published his groundbreaking essay "As We May Think" in *The Atlantic Monthly.* The editors of the magazine marveled at Bush's premise, which might well be called a manifesto for connectional intelligence. They wrote that, after the weapons of war have been put down,

> . . . men [and women] of science should then turn to the massive task of making more accessible our bewildering store of knowledge. For years inventions have extended man's physical powers rather than the powers of his mind. Trip hammers that multiply the fists, microscopes that sharpen the eye, and engines of destruction and detection are new results, but not the end results, of modern science. Now, says Dr. Bush, instruments are at hand which, if properly developed, will give man access to and command over the inherited knowledge of the ages.[1]

We believe that we are now unlocking what those editors called, nearly seventy years ago, "our bewildering store of knowledge," because today, for the first time in history, billions of people from all walks of life, races, countries and social economic status are inclusively connected. Previously, new forms of connection and communications were primarily reserved for and used by the elite. Never before have so many people had access, through mobile, social and digital technology, to so much data, knowledge and collective brainpower. We believe that this connectedness gives us power to solve big problems, turn dreams into realities, create amazing products, upgrade survival to prosperity, change social policy, discover life-saving medical cures and much, much more. When we combine this with the inclusive imagination and insight of billions of people—all connected—we begin to comprehend the monster wave of connectional intelligence that is transforming our lives.

Here's what we think is happening. We all know about the value of having high IQ, but historically, the importance of high intelligence rose after the advent of the printing press, when people could share ideas in the form of reading and books. This led to rapid advances in science,

Never before have so many people had access,
through mobile, social and digital technology,
to so much collective brain power.

widespread literacy, new forms of governance and the many inventions that brought us to the modern world.

Similarly, the importance of EQ (emotional intelligence) rose dramatically with the rise of large, densely populated cities and as organizations with thousands of people spread across the globe. Having high EQ is always valuable to leaders, but when leading large groups, it becomes a critical capability. Indeed, today, in both the private and nonprofit sectors, high EQ is recognized as a must-have ability for anyone seeking to lead a large, diverse and geographically dispersed organization.

And now, we are seeing the rise of something we call connectional intelligence (CxQ). Our definition: Connectional Intelligence is the ability to combine the world's diversity of people, networks, disciplines and resources, forging connections that create value, meaning and breakthrough results.

For us, the promise of connectional intelligence couldn't be simpler, more powerful or more inspiring:

Take a Dream.
Add Connection.
Dream Bigger.
Get Big Things Done.

The word *connection* gets thrown around a lot today. Faced with an abundance of tools for connecting, we are often left overwhelmed, without a clear sense of how to use the myriad forms of connection in the service of human potential. To some people, "connection" simply means being constantly online: social media, technology, apps, entertainment, digital sharing and all the forms of instant communication that are becoming a pervasive part of the fabric of how we live.

Connectional intelligence is the ability to combine the world's diversity of people, networks, disciplines and resources, forging connections that create value, meaning and breakthrough results.

For those of you who think connectional intelligence sounds good, but feel that you don't need to be more connected than you already are, know that we're talking about something much broader and more profound than a new-and-cool set of digital tools. And for those of you who think that hyper-connectivity is just about teenagers on Twitter and twenty-somethings on Instagram, know that inclusive connection is the foundation on which the next wave of human potential will rise.

Humans have always been connectional. We've always been curious. We've always combined things. We've always been travelers. We've always been conversationalists. We are living in a new era in which the traditional routes to power—the schools you go to, the contacts in your address book, the families you are born to—are no longer the only ways to get ahead. Never before have so many people, of so many different backgrounds, been able to connect with such a vast network of ideas, information and resources. One of the key things to understand is that connectional intelligence combined with inclusive connection is inherently democratic.

One of the questions that we seek to address in this book is how do you cut through the noise of e-mail and social media to connect *intelligently?* How do we marshal what we know that much more quickly? How do we find and keep supporters? How do we influence the greatest number of people? How do we propel connectional intelligence beyond traditional networking and the massive entertainment element of our digital lives toward a loftier purpose? In short, how do we get behind this newfound connectivity and use it to get to the places where we want to go?

Two decades after the Internet blasted into our collective lives, it's time for a guidebook that shows us all how to access and launch this innate human capability to make connections. The big news, especially for anyone who's experienced digital overload or fatigue, is that there are many real-life applications for all of your connectedness that are bigger and more powerful than how many followers you have on Twitter or how many likes your post gets on Facebook. Connectional intelligence propels us all beyond networking and entertainment toward a loftier purpose—improving people's lives, building sustainable societies and creating the futures we want. Soon it will also be a required skill: today's and tomorrow's generations will know no world without smart connection, and we can't ask them to park or squander what they do best.

Connectional intelligence is bigger and more powerful than how many followers you have on Twitter or how many likes your post gets on Facebook.

So what does this look like in our modern world? A few examples of connectional intelligence at work (and at play) are discussed below.

It's used by Ben Kaufman, CEO and founder of the company Quirky, to help average, everyday people bring their inventions to life. In just a few short years, Ben has shepherded hundreds of inventors through the process of developing, manufacturing and distributing hundreds of products into major retail outlets such as Best Buy, Home Depot and Williams-Sonoma. Quirky's recent ad campaign shows how it upends traditional corporate structures and attitudes. In a series of ads called, "The World's Least Important CEO," Ben underscores that it's the team, not the boss, that matters. In one of the ads, he posts his phone number and promises that "The World's Least Important CEO Is Not Too Busy to Take Your Call." When one media reporter called and got Ben himself, she was so stunned that she hung up. When the reporter's friend called to pitch an idea, Ben gave the budding inventor two minutes of his time, offering advice about how to get a product into Home Depot.[2] For a CEO of even a small company to post his phone number, share his personal e-mail (Ben does that too), and still manage to get big things done rewrites (or at least revises) the rules of leadership in a significant way. We'll be talking more about Quirky later in this book.

Nike believes that the best way to stimulate environmentally sustainable innovation is through connectional intelligence. This is evident in Nike's GreenXchange (GX), a web-based marketplace where companies can collaborate and share intellectual property to foster new environmentally sustainable business models and innovation.[3] Nike took the substantial risk of making available on GX more than four hundred of its own patents for public research. The risk paid off. Soon enough, a mountain-biking company used a rubber patent to innovate their tire inner tubes, thus bringing a greener product to market more quickly and cheaply than the manufacturer could on its own.

Using its MyStarbucks platform, Starbucks tasked its loyal fans to come up with new product and service innovations. Within five years customers presented 150,000 new ideas. One of the first of these consumer-centric designs that Starbucks rolled out was a little green combination swizzle stick/stopper that keeps hot coffee from burning your fingers and does away with the need for flat lids with holes in them.[4]

That's connectional intelligence at work: elegant solutions, created by the kind of broad-based outreach that could only be possible in our age of inclusive connection, brought to market quickly and decisively by a diverse but unified group, working collaboratively toward a common goal.

Just a few years ago, there had never been a nationally ranked pro surfer from Maui—in surfing circles, Hawaii's second-largest island was considered something of a joke—but Dusty Payne, a young surfing fanatic, wanted to change all that. Rounding up four local surfing buddies who believed that, as a group, they could help each other become great, the five boys vowed to learn as much as they could by competing against and critiquing one another.[5]

They carried out frame-by-frame analyses of DVD and YouTube videos of the top surfers, skateboarders, windsurfers, mountain bikers and motor-cross champions on the planet, and spent hours comparing their own filmed techniques against them. Combining ideas that came from connections to adjacent sports and competitors, Dusty came up with his own signature "Superman" move, a key factor in helping him win a world junior surfing championship. Today Dusty and his pals are all nationally ranked pros—and Maui is finally on the map as a surfing incubator.

Most powerfully, connectional intelligence can, and does, save lives and improve the quality of life for people who need it most. It was by using the tools and tenets of connectional intelligence that a ragtag group in Boston helped the United Nations, the Coast Guard and the Marines rescue thousands of survivors of the 2010 Haitian earthquake. It was connectional intelligence that inspired one woman to petition Victoria's Secret to begin manufacturing a "mastectomy bra," hoping to aid the thousands of women like her mother, a breast cancer survivor. And it's connectional intelligence that's helping Harvard Medical School researchers come up with solutions that are raising the bar on care and treatment of people living with Type 1 diabetes.

As co-authors, we've now spent the last few years riding the wave of connectional intelligence together. The exciting news is that we found it everywhere we looked: in corporations and in public schools, in agriculture and sports, in the United States and around the world. We didn't invent it, and we're not trying to can it. It's as old as tribal wisdom and as ever-changing as the models of your favorite handheld device. This book isn't about the "25 Most Connectionally Intelligent People" in the world. It's not a who's who or a greatest hits list. It's a guidebook for people from all walks of life who want to get big things done.

The stories we present ask and answer the question: What can anyone and everyone accomplish when they connect intelligently? At the core of our work is the knowledge that these stories of how men and women (and sometimes kids) are making these huge intellectual and creative leaps aren't just one-offs. Connectional intelligence is more than the cool YouTube video of someone doing something amazing; it's more than viral, crowd-sourced campaigns, or one out-the-box company that created something brand new. The very way we do business is changing. The way we're learning is changing. We cannot get where we want to go, as creative individuals and as innovative companies, if we view these "oh wow" stories in isolation. They need to be understood as a very exciting, very powerful, new whole.

This book isn't about the "25 Most Connectionally Intelligent People" in the world. It's not a who's who or a greatest hits list. It's about what anyone and everyone can accomplish when they connect intelligently.

So how did this book get started?

Perhaps in today's world of hyper-connectivity, it was almost inevitable that we would connect. When we first met, what jumped out at us right away was that despite our generational differences, we had a lot to talk about: Saj-nicole was in the midst of doing work she loves. As CEO of Cambridge International Group, she serves as a confidential advisor and thinking partner to CEOs around the world, helping them work through their most difficult challenges; Erica was a fellow at Harvard's Center for Public Leadership. Today, as CEO of Cotential, she works with organizations to drive innovation across cultures and generations to prepare the global workforce for the future. The generational differences were real: One of us got her start as the first woman to join the faculty of MIT's applied mathematics department. (How long ago was that? Back then, there were no women's bathrooms in MIT's entire mathematics building.) The other started off as a young social change leader when she was named to *Teen People* magazine's "20 Teens Who Will Change the World." (By then, bathrooms in many colleges were co-ed.) Our generational differences were real but so was a common strand that we recognized in each other's work. We were both committed to the ideal of helping people get big things done and felt that our moment in history offered more opportunity for more types of people than ever before. The question became: How can we inspire and teach people everywhere to harness connectional intelligence in order to live and work that much better?

One of the discoveries that surprised us is that connectional intelligence works across all personality types. You might think, at first, that it requires an outgoing personality—someone who loves networking, real-life socializing and being known, and who values a stage and media presence. But we've seen that this is not the only type of person who accesses profound connectional intelligence to get big things done. The self-described introvert who finds it difficult to introduce himself to strangers at a networking conference might establish a blog presence online and then extend these online relationships into the real world.

Today, you can source energy and capacity from different forms of connection—like extroverts, you can start from networks of people to spark ideas that then mobilize more people. But also, like introverts, you can draw from different sources like books, nature and music that then form the basis of relationships that generate more ideas and possibilities. If connectional intelligence was merely about traditional networking, only extroverts would excel at it. But connectional intelligence is built on a use of technology and traditional forms of information, as well as an emotional intelligence, which makes it a resource that introverts can tap into as well. In connectional intelligence, the big picture and big ideas matter as much as how well you sell yourself in a meeting or in a professional setting.

We've seen this in our own work and life. Saj-nicole is the classic "Renaissance" thinker when it comes to connectional intelligence. She starts by learning from every field, and it is the pull of ideas that prompts her to meet people. As an integrative thinker, it has often been her connected thinking, sourced from the arts, humanities, sports and science, that fuels her biggest business ideas and leads her to connections with people to get big things done. Erica started more as an outside-in thinker: her initial connection to people sparks her curiosity, creating new ideas, which in turn mobilize more people to get big things done. This kind of thinking was shown when Erica co-hosted gatherings with hundreds of young professionals in New York on social entrepreneurship. The events led to a broader team of young professionals who took the next step in co-creating NY+acumen, a local community of social change leaders in New York in partnership with Acumen, a nonprofit that raises charitable donations to invest in companies, leaders and ideas that are changing the way the world tackles poverty. The initial pilot was a success and the +Acumen network, led by Acumen's Jo-Ann Tan, is now a global community of social change leaders in over 26 cities.

When it comes to getting big things done in organizations, we urge managers and senior leaders to fully encourage the connectional intelligence of introverts and remember to avoid situations in which over-collaboration and over-connection kill creativity and allow groupthink to take over. Being connectionally intelligent is just as much about understanding when and how to work alone as it is about knowing how to collaborate.

This book is divided into three parts. Part One introduces our story and the concept of connectional intelligence. Part Two is a collection of stories that exhibits the breadth and potential of connectional intelligence. Taken together, these stories give you a panoramic view of how connectional intelligence adds possibility to all aspects of our lives, work and society. These are stories about real people who have accomplished things that would not have been imaginable a generation ago, or even—in some cases—five years ago. We think you'll see yourself in at least a few of these stories and, possibly, in many. As we've shared these stories in our work, consulting with CEOs, executives, boards and organizations, we've seen again and again how the stories aren't merely inspiring: they're practical and applicable. The spark they create is both immediate and useful. Part Three is all about you, the reader. It's a handbook to guide you in using connectional intelligence to power your dreams, in your work and in your life.

One of the core elements of connectional intelligence is a fundamentally cross-generational, know-the-rules-and-*then*-break-them ethos. The new tech-savvy generation is unleashing its connectional intelligence and is not willing to wait until the older generations leave power. But they also cannot fix things alone; they need the knowledge, experience and wisdom of the older generation. If we want to go fast to solve our most pressing challenges, we all have to come together in connectionally intelligent ways to use everything we have.

> *If you remember nothing else from this book, remember this: connectional intelligence is the best, most efficient, most powerful way to supersize any dream.*

In the journey that resulted in this book, we've lived this. It hasn't always been easy. But we have emerged as a cross-generational team in which both of us have been transformed, able to do so much more together than if we had stayed in our respective generational spheres. We meet at the intersection of our generations and our perspectives; we embody connectional intelligence in almost everything we do. We both believe that if more people and organizations harnessed the force of connectional intelligence, they'd radically transform how they live and work now and in the future.

What we know, for sure, is that connectional intelligence is an un-stoppable force available to all of us. We hope you'll find this book an inspiring, engaging read—and an opportunity to connect the dots be-tween groups and individuals who are getting big things done using the same social media tools and technology we all use every day.

But the real power of this book, we believe, will come later. After you've read the last chapter, when you're at home or at work, in your car or on vacation, and something sparks. Maybe there's something you want to create. Or maybe something unthinkable is happening and you want to help or inspire others to join with you to make a change. Maybe you have a business problem and you know that you need more brains at the metaphorical boardroom table and you remember a connectional intelligence story that helps you figure out how to get big things done. If you remember nothing else from this book, remember this: connectional intelligence is the best, most efficient, most powerful way to supersize any dream.

We believe that harnessing connectional intelligence calls on us, individually and collectively, to go on what writer and mythologist Joseph Campbell named the "hero's journey."[6]

As Campbell and others defined it, a hero's journey typically begins with a need or inspiration, followed by a call to adventure, the crossing of a threshold, a joining-in of accomplices, a road of trials, a confrontation, an apotheosis and a return threshold, until at last the hero, or heroine, becomes "the master of two worlds."[7]

Whether you're an individual or part of a team, like the hero's journey, your road toward connectional intelligence will also begin with passion, and then you will make a decision, assemble accomplices, face down barriers and boundaries until you finally accomplish your goal.

If you could multiply what you know in your head and your heart by the power of everyone you could contact, what would you do?

Understanding connectional intelligence is only the first step of your hero's journey. To accomplish what the men and women in this book have done takes dedication, courage, perseverance and, sometimes, luck.

We want to ask you a question now that we'll return to at the end of the book: If you could multiply what you know in your head and your heart, your IQ and EQ, by the power of everyone you've ever e-mailed or could contact by social media and other technology, what would you do? Which is, of course, to say, if you could do *anything*, what would you do?

2

THE ROOTS OF CONNECTIONAL INTELLIGENCE

WHEN WE BEGAN TO MAP THE WORLD OF CONNECTIONAL intelligence, we understood that the ability to make breakthroughs by combining ideas, people, information and resources was nothing new. Leonardo da Vinci, painter and architect, mathematician and inventor, botanist and renowned polymath, may well be considered the godfather of connectional intelligence.

Florence Nightingale, the mother of modern nursing, first rose to global prominence during the Crimean War. She was known to the wounded soldiers she tended during her nighttime rounds as the "Lady with the Lamp." But it was really her connectional intelligence that led Nightingale to the discoveries that not only saved lives, but ensured her lasting legacies in both mathematics and medicine.

Born in Florence, Italy to a wealthy and well-connected British family, Florence Nightingale had the good fortune of having a father who believed in the education of women and made his daughters' schooling a high priority. She was tutored, largely by her father, in the subjects of Italian, Greek, Latin, history and mathematics. Nightingale felt an early push to the field of nursing, although her mother and sisters thought women need not pursue a career. She is reputed to have turned down at least one advantageous marriage proposal for fear that marriage would prevent her from doing her life's work. It was not until she was in her thirties, when the pressure to marry had lessened, that she undertook her first major position as superintendent at the Institute for the Care of Sick Gentlewomen in London.

A few months later, she took more than three dozen volunteer nurses—most of whom she had trained—to Balaklava in Crimea. There she discovered that unsanitary conditions and unregulated medical practices were causing unspeakable suffering and high mortality rates among the wounded soldiers in the British camp. At the time, the military doctors were scrambling to decrease the death rate, as one out of two wounded soldiers died in the camp hospitals. Using the advanced mathematical training she had received from her father, Nightingale collected data on the unsanitary conditions and showed how her methods might decrease the mortality rate. She is credited with creating the first polar area diagram and was a pioneer in the use of graphics to display statistical data. While she was making her case to the doctors and military officials on the ground, she also deployed a letter campaign to the press and to government officials back home. (A letter-writing campaign is an important precursor to our modern-day social media campaigns.) Nightingale's letter writing led the British government to commission the design and building of one of the world's first pre-fab hospitals, Renkoi Hospital. At Renkoi, the mortality rate for wounded soldiers dropped more than 90 percent.[1]

In her later years, Nightingale took what she had learned about statistics, sanitary conditions and public health service to India, where her work led to a dramatic decrease in the death rate of wounded soldiers, from 69 dead in 1,000 to 18 in 1,000.[2] Nightingale was the first woman inducted into the Royal Statistical Society.[3]

While her moniker, the Lady with the Lamp, is an eternal part of Nightingale's mythology, where she truly shed the greatest light was by showing how data, analysis, sharing information and everyday citizens' campaigning could result in positive change. The campaign she started for better, more sanitary hospitals led to important evolutions in medicine and public health not just in her native England, but all around the world.[4]

You can also see the exponential power of connectional intelligence in the story of Benjamin Franklin's trust. At his death, Franklin bequeathed £1000 to the cities of Boston, where he was born, and Philadelphia, where he lived. Nearly two hundred years later, the Philadelphia Franklin Trust was worth over two million dollars, and the Boston Trust was worth over five million dollars. The money provided college scholarships and mortgage loans and funded the building and endowment of Franklin Institutes in each city.[5] But the original connectional intelligence spark can be seen in the genesis of the idea: in 1785, a French mathematician named Charles Joseph Mathon de la Coeur wrote a book called *Fortunate Richard,* which introduced the idea of a smallish philanthropic fund that would grow in interest over not dozens, but hundreds of years. *Fortunate Richard* was meant to be a friendly parody of Franklin's "Poor Richard's Almanack," but instead it inspired Franklin to dream big, add connection, dream bigger and get big things done.[6]

We could add hundreds of names to the list of those who have used connectional intelligence to spark change—including civil rights activist Rosa Parks, architect Maya Lin, Nelson Mandela (who we'll talk more about later) and former President Bill Clinton—but this isn't a book about luminaries, it's a book about everyday people who have done extraordinary things. It's a book about you, me and the power of us. It's a book about the power of what happens when people connect and dreams collide.

Connectional intelligence is the kind of genius that begins with a conversation. More specifically, a question: Have you noticed this particular thing? What have you found in your work/research/heart/experience/explorations? Do you know someone who might be able to help me? What works in your area of expertise? Could I try that in mine? What if we got together and ran an experiment, started a clinical trial, did something different, unexpected, something that failed once but might just work this time?

The American educator Deborah Meier, who many credit as being the founder of the modern small-schools movement, said that "We come out of the womb questioning." Yet, as Warren Berger notes in his book *A More Beautiful Question,* most of us reach our questioning peak at the age of four or five.[7] After that, we become more focused on the answers, and all the gold stars associated with getting the right answers, than on the beauty of the questions. Berger explains that it can be easy to get lost in the spin cycle of "why" or the rabbit hole of information that makes Google such a powerful, but also limited, tool. He states that in order to flex and develop what he calls our internal "inquiry" app, we have to question with focus and intention. "To question productively and 'beautifully' is to inquire with direction and purpose."[8]

A questioner can move forward on almost any problem or challenge by first trying to understand it (What is the problem?); then imagining possible solutions (What if I came at the problem this way, or that way?); then pondering the value of a new solution (Does it matter enough to commit heart and mind to doing something new, different, and possibly risky?); and finally trying to figure out practical ways to turn those what-if ideas and possibilities into realities (How might I actually begin to make this happen?).

> *Connectional intelligence is the kind of genius that begins with a conversation. What? What if? Does it matter? How do we get this big thing done?*

Questioning is a path followed again and again by the connectionally intelligent subjects we discuss in this book. Whether they were trying to figure out how to get medical supplies to patients in the middle of massive civil unrest, or trying to figure out how to grow the world's first 2,000-pound pumpkin, they began by asking pointed and purposeful questions:

- *What* is the problem?
- *What if* I engaged the resources, information, people and ideas at my disposal in another way?
- *Does it matter?* To me? To others? To the future?
- *How* might I get this big thing done?

More than a decade ago, Malcolm Gladwell published his landmark book, *The Tipping Point,* in which he described something that he called the "law of the few": "The success of any kind of social epidemic is heavily dependent on the involvement of people with a particular and rare set of social gifts."[9] (W. E. B. DuBois described a similar phenomenon in 1903, with *his* groundbreaking essay, "The Talented Tenth.")

The few described in the "law of the few" were broken into three categories: connectors, mavens and salesmen. But it was really the first group, the connectors, that captured our global imagination. After the go-go 80s and the first internet boom of the 90s, most of us were underwhelmed by people who were merely great at networking. A connector, on the other hand, was someone special. As Gladwell describes them, they "are the people in a community who know large numbers of people and who are in the habit of making introductions. A connector is essentially the social equivalent of a computer network hub. They usually know people across an array of social, cultural, professional, and economic circles, and make a habit of introducing people who work or live in different circles. They are people who link us up with the world . . . people with a special gift for bringing the world together."[10]

What is interesting, as we look back on Gladwell's work today, is that we can see that millennials, as a generation, have become both hyper-connected and gifted connectors. And, today, no matter how old you are, inclusive connection is not only about entertainment or news; it is embedded in daily life. We do everything in a connected space, from sharing our lives with friends and family (who may live in different cities or countries), to shopping and paying bills, communicating at work, meeting people after work, finding places to get a decent burrito, competing at sports and games, accessing health care, learning new things, or taking care of children and aging parents, ad infinitum. And our online connections have accelerated our insatiable curiosity to connect offline.

More than a decade after *The Tipping Point* came out, it has been exciting, gratifying and inspiring for us to realize that we've moved way, way past the law of the few into a territory that our parents and our grandparents could only have imagined: "the potential of many." This is not to undercut the vision of our ancestors. One suspects that when Ben Franklin bequeathed £1,000 to the cities of Philadelphia and Boston, he saw his gift as an investment in the "potential of many." And when Nelson Mandela convened the Truth and Reconciliation committees, that was also an investment in the "potential of many." We are confident that

Rosa Parks sat down to stand up because she believed in the potential of many as well.

For a nineteenth-century woman, Florence Nightingale traveled extensively. Her writings on what she saw rival the great travel writing of noted authors such as Freya Stark and Henry James. When Nightingale visited Egypt in 1850, she adventurously traveled up the Nile to the temples of Abu Simbel and wrote: "I don't think I have ever seen anything which affected me much more than this . . . Sublime in the highest style of intellectual beauty, intellect without effort, without suffering . . . It makes the impression upon one that thousands of voices do, uniting in one unanimous simultaneous feeling of enthusiasm or emotion, which is said to overcome the strongest man."[11] One of Nightingale's gifts, it is clear, was her ability to see—in everything she did and everywhere she visited—the power of connection, the uniting of thousands of voices, to create and transform the world we live in.

It was with our own collective history in mind that we came together to write this book and begin the work of studying, mapping, researching and coaching the lessons of connectional intelligence. Yet, the very thing that makes us strong as a pair can make it challenging to create one shared vision on the page. It's not easy to form a partnership across differences. We differ in age and ethnicity, in life experience and sometimes in worldview. It takes work, it takes guts and it takes a patient kind of commitment. It takes willingness, stamina and honesty to make the inherent tensions of diversity and difference productive.

Early in our journey, we came across the example of restaurateurs Yotam Ottolenghi and Sami Tamimi. The partnership of these two men is well-known, and what made their story compelling to us is their partnership across differences. Two men, one Israeli, one Palestinian, each born in Jerusalem just months after the Six Day War. They met in London, where they had both migrated and made their way through the culinary world. When they met, they spoke in English, then in Hebrew. But even still, it took a while for Yotam to recognize that his new friend, Sami, was Palestinian, since he spoke Hebrew with no accent. Yotam and Sami opened their first restaurant in Notting Hill in 2002, and from the beginning it was a love of great food, a shared Mediterranean-inspired palate, not the politics and the tortured history of their people, that brought them together.[12] Their story inspired ours—it's not every day that a math prodigy turned acclaimed global business leader from Cambridge becomes friends and co-author with an Indian-American leadership expert from New York, New Delhi and Pittsburgh.

A decade after Yotam and Sami started their restaurant, the BBC approached them about writing a cookbook—and making a documentary about Jerusalem. They realized that they were being asked to take on a project that would challenge them at the core of their differences, but it would also give them the opportunity to create together on a whole new level. They approached the project with a healthy dose of trepidation and skepticism.

They started with the questions of "what?" and "what if?" The turning point in their decision on whether to do the project was when they faced the "does it matter?" question. The reason to go back to Jerusalem was the same reason that African Americans make pilgrimages to the slave ports of Gorée Island. Such a trip says "I'm willing to take it all in"; the knot of pain and loss that has been pulled tight for hundreds of years, the moments that are decidedly not (depending on your generation) Kodak or Instagram-worthy, the deep knowledge that can only come from venturing forth in person rather than connecting remotely via Skype or other technological means. The Jerusalem documentary was an opportunity to do this, not just for themselves, but for many people. To shed light, through both the literal and metaphorical breaking of bread, on how food is a powerful and unusually peaceful strand that unites communities in a part of the world that remains so dangerously divided.

By doing the documentary, the two men could create connections and new perspectives on Jerusalem for the people of Israel and Palestine, and for all the people who loved their food all over the world. When Yotam and Sami decided to return to Jerusalem, they were saying, on a deep soul level, "We're ready. We are all in."

We've seen powerful parallels between our journey and the work that Yotam and Sami have done together, from London to Jerusalem. As we've worked together to forge the language, perspective, platform and tools that comprise this book, our efforts to connect have elevated our connectional intelligence. Our differences move from foreground to background when we focus on what we have in common: unrelenting optimism about the potential of everyday people to get big things done. Each of us holds half of what's needed. Because of both our shared commitment and our differences, we are able to see, understand and activate our connectional intelligence in a way that neither of us could when we stood alone. And together, we want to help you to do the same.

Connectional intelligence comes alive when you connect to individuals who share your vision who say, "We're ready. We're all in."

Connectional intelligence can be experienced in so many different ways: it's a wave, it's a seed of an idea that is going to grow into a 2,000-pound pumpkin, it's a table on which people of different faiths and ethnicities break bread and share ideas, it's a workbench where modern-day Ben Franklins (hello Ben Kaufman and the Quirky crew) invent the things the world needs, and it's a computer screen where ten seconds of your time helps to digitize two and a half million books a year. Connectional intelligence is both as ancient as Jerusalem and as brand new as a microchip.

E. M. Forster famously wrote: "Only connect! Only connect the prose and the passion and both will be exalted, and human love will be seen at its height."[13] We might well say about connectional intelligence: "Connect intelligently! Connect with purpose and passion and human potential will be seen at its height."

These stories have enriched our view of ourselves and of our collective human potential. They've helped us to connect the dots in bigger, more powerful ways. As we go about the business of advising CEOs, companies, communities and causes about how to get big things done, connectional intelligence enriches the narrative. It allows us to be who we've always been—smart, curious, passionate about achievement but also passionate about inclusion—while at the same time, it gives us dozens of new road maps of how to tackle the tasks at hand, how to get big things done.

Connect intelligently! Connect with purpose and passion and human potential will be seen at its height.

We invite you to view the stories in this book as a tasting menu of modern achievement and possibility. Our simple manifesto is: take a dream, add connection, dream bigger, get big things done. We've shared the stories in this book, and our take on them, with hundreds of people, from CEOs to human resources execs, from nongovernmental organization (NGO) workers to public policy makers. There's a story for every individual who is striving to look at a problem with fresh eyes. There's inspiration, sustenance and strategy for every person who is trying to architect her or his own dream. It's not a gimmick or a trend. A fairy doesn't get her wings and we don't make a dollar every time someone uses the phrase "connectional intelligence."

It's as ancient as Renaissance-era Florence, where Leonardo da Vinci, a boy born out of wedlock to a notary public and a peasant woman, was able to get the education and the exposure that would allow him to create not only the most famous painting of all time, but also dozens of inventions, and to map not only the human anatomy, but also an early version of plate tectonics that described how layers of the earth moved in relation to each other, hundreds of years before scientists could give such a theory a name, much less continue the work of defining and refining tectonic theory.

Connectional intelligence is Ben Franklin throwing £1,000 not toward his sons, or their sons, but two hundred years into the future, with the understanding that small sums, given with great vision and hope, could indeed truly get big things done. It's Rosa Parks sitting down on the bus. It's Nelson Mandela standing up for prisoners and prison guards, seeing that both groups were bound and enslaved by the system of apartheid, and then carving a path out of a barbarian history into a present that is, while not perfect, a model of economic stability and educational possibility for an entire continent.

We invite you to view the stories in this book as a tasting menu of modern achievement and possibility.

As we've gathered these stories, held them up to the light and committed to paper what we see, we've tried to be mindful of what Da Vinci advised when he developed what he called "the principles for the development of a complete mind." He said, "Study the science of art. Study the art of science. Develop your senses—especially learn how to see. Realize that everything connects to everything else."[14]

We go forth, connected, always growing, changing and asking what we hope are the beautiful questions, in service of doing this work together.

PART 2

3

HOW TO GET BIG THINGS DONE

A Primer

SO WHO CARES ABOUT GIANT PUMPKINS? MAYBE A FEW thousand people who grow them competitively in places like Palmer, Alaska; Half Moon Bay, California; and East Hamlet, Indiana. We were definitely in the pumpkin-agnostic category before we heard the story of Ron Wallace, the first man to grow a one-ton pumpkin. But it turns out that what you learn from growing a massive pumpkin can help solve hunger and starvation around the world.

Growing super-sized pumpkins may sound like an unusual hobby, but it's surprisingly popular. There are giant pumpkin clubs. There is a giant pumpkin website that gets more daily visitors than some national news sites. There are annual giant pumpkin competitions, with ribbons and cash awards. And then there is obsession. Consider: Farming began around 10,000 BC. It took until the year 2000 for a farmer to grow the first thousand-pound pumpkin. Ron Wallace hoped to double that weight a mere decade later.[1]

In the ultra-niche world of pumpkin farming, growing a one-ton pumpkin has long been considered a kind of loony dream. The average pumpkin weighs between ten and twenty pounds, and the growing season lasts anywhere between seventy-five and one hundred days. It turns out that way back in 1959, when Charles Schulz first began drawing the iconic Charlie Brown comic strips about an elusive hero called the Great Pumpkin, he knew something that most people don't: pumpkins are temperamental. And needy. They hate cold weather, have to be watered constantly and do best in enriched soil where their vines can twist and snake out into nearby areas. They're ill-equipped to handle frosts, root damage or insect infestations. Half of all pumpkins die before reaching maturity.

Yet Ron Wallace, a full-time country club manager and second-generation pumpkin enthusiast (his dad grew big pumpkins too), managed to beat all the odds and do the seemingly impossible. How? Connectional intelligence.

TAKE A DREAM. ADD CONNECTION.

Almost ten years before his giant pumpkin landed him in the *Guinness World Records*, Ron became obsessed with a book called *How to Grow World-Class Giant Pumpkins*. He soon joined a statewide pumpkin association and, around the same time, stumbled upon the website Bigpumpkins.com. Online and off, he started exchanging pumpkin trivia, war stories, strategies and best practices with other growers. He reached out to potato and tomato farmers, curious whether they had any insights that might aid him in his quest. He badgered well-known scientists for agricultural advice and information. He shipped his pumpkin plants off to experts for testing. And along the way, he

stumbled across something called *mycorrhizal fungi*—naturally oc-
curring underground spores that attach to a plant's root system and
bring water and nutrients back to the plant—which he added to his
arsenal.[2]

At this point, Ron was devoting up to forty hours a week reading
books, writing articles and researching the best way to bring his colossus
to life. (There are shades of Malcolm Gladwell's 10,000 hours theory
here and in many connectional intelligence stories.) But it was not all
about the hours. Some of his best discoveries happened by accident. For
example, forgetting to add nutrients in his soil in early April, he rushed
to add them in late May, which likely contributed to the massive growth
spurt of his giant pumpkin. In his search for information, Ron learned
that potato farmers use a technique called biofumigation, in which the
soil is leavened with manure to help protect against pests and disease.
When Ron tried it, he found that the resulting high mustard content
in the soil created sturdier crops. Armed with what he now knew, Ron
mixed and matched techniques taken from familiar and faraway disciplines and industries. A little of this, a little of that. The result was a
pumpkin that he dubbed The Freak II. It was a sprawling, un-beautiful
thing, more yellow than orange, but it became the world's first one-ton
pumpkin at the 2012 Topsfield, Massachusetts agricultural fair and,
with that, Ron Wallace made history.[3]

ADD CONNECTION. DREAM BIGGER.
GET BIG THINGS DONE.

We're the first to admit that stories and videos like the tale of the one-
ton pumpkin show up almost daily in our in-boxes and in our Facebook
and Twitter news feeds. So, besides the fact that Ron Wallace is the kind
of underdog champ who makes us all feel like we can dream the impossible dream, why does a giant pumpkin matter?

It matters because Ron's story is an almost textbook illustration of connectional intelligence. It began as a solo act. Then Ron joined forces with groups—local growers, national growers, scientists and soil experts. Diversity played a natural role in Ron's research process. He wasn't sure that potato and tomato farmers had anything to teach him, but technology made it easy for him to get as many different kinds of brains on his project as possible, at virtually no cost. Because of this, Ron combined ideas and disciplines in ways that no one in his field ever had done before. There was also an element of courage: Ron pestered the smartest scientists he could find with his questions. Many wouldn't give him the time of day, but the ones who did take a moment to answer an e-mail and offer advice represented an intellectual resource to which, fifty years ago, a guy like Ron would have never had access. Moreover, almost everyone who contributed intellectual brainpower to the growth of Freak II did so for *free*. They weren't paid. They weren't courted by the glory of the project or the celebrity of the one who pursued them. They offered up their connectional intelligence because they were inspired by Ron's curiosity, his commitment and his passion.

The story would all be enormously instructive even if it ended there, but it doesn't. Seven thousand miles away from Ron's hometown of Greene, Rhode Island, scientists and farmers took note of the many media reports about the Freak II. In India, where more than half of all workers are employed in agriculture, officials have begun experimenting with Ron's techniques, with the goal of producing more and bigger crops in less time and with less chemicals. Big industrial agriculture is taking notice too.[4] In other words, a monster fruit grown by a hobbyist Rhode Island pumpkin farmer is, right at this very moment, influencing the future of large-scale agriculture, food production and potentially the global food supply. Connectional intelligence doesn't get much better than that.

THE COURAGE TO ASK THE HARD QUESTIONS

Ron Wallace's connectional intelligence inspired him to ask unprecedented questions. Inclusive connectivity gave him the ability to ask those questions to literally anyone in the world, creating a list of resources that would have been unimaginable a generation ago.

The same mix of connectional intelligence, question-asking and inclusive connectivity is at the heart of how an unknown graduate student upended research that had been embraced and lauded by a generation of economists, members of Congress and other public policy members.

In 2009, twenty-eight-year-old Thomas Herndon was a nobody. A graduate of Evergreen State College in Olympia, Washington, he was doing his graduate work in economics at the University of Massachusetts in Amherst. In a third-year course, his professors gave the students an assignment: pick an economics paper, replicate the results. Thomas chose "Growth in a Time of Debt," by Carmen Reinhart and Ken Rogoff.

To his surprise, he could not replicate their findings.

Carmen Reinhart, a professor at Harvard and former chief economist at Bear Stearns, was known for her ability, in her own words, to round up data, "like cattle, all over the plain."[5] Carmen Reinhart was at the pinnacle of data mining—it was the cornerstone of her reputation. The paper's co-author, Harvard professor Ken Rogoff, had similar sterling credentials: he was the former chief of the International Monetary Fund. So how could their data possibly be wrong?

"I felt really bad about it," Thomas Herndon recalled. "I thought I had likely made a gross error. Because I'm a student, the odds were I was the one who'd made the mistake, not the well-known Harvard professors."[6]

His professors agreed.

"I remember I had a meeting with my professor, Michael Ash, where he basically said, 'Come on, Tom, this isn't too hard—you just gotta go sort this out.'"[7]

So he kept at it, e-mailing Reinhart and Rogoff to request their data.

When he got their spreadsheets, he was stunned—in a key calculation, Reinhart and Rogoff had only included fifteen of the twenty countries they analyzed. They'd left out Australia, Austria, Belgium, Canada and Denmark. And the numbers for one bad year from New Zealand—a small economy—were given the same weight as the numbers for twenty years from the United Kingdom.

Thomas's conclusion: "Coding errors, selective exclusion of available data, and unconventional weighting of summary statistics lead to serious errors that inaccurately represent the relationship between public debt and GDP growth among twenty advanced economies in the post-war period."[8]

This was not a small, obscure conclusion. Many economists had used Reinhart and Rogoff's findings to argue that the way out of the then-current recession was not increased government spending—as during the New Deal in the American Depression of the 1930s—but less. That is, austerity. Many politicians accepted that argument as gospel: austerity-driven policy helped drive the unemployment rate to over ten percent for the eurozone as a whole, and more than twenty percent in Greece and Spain.[9] That's a mistake with consequences, mostly for the poor or unemployed.

One of Thomas's professors, Robert Pollin, didn't believe the graduate student, at first: "I thought, 'Ok, he's a student. He's got to be wrong.' These are eminent economists and he's a graduate student. So we pushed him and we pushed him and pushed him and after about a month of pushing him, I said, 'Goddamn, he's right.'"[10]

In collaboration with his professors, Thomas published his findings, as a working draft, on the Political Economy Research Institute website.

Ignition was instant: the website crashed. Paul Krugman, CNBC and other media figures and outlets took notice. "It was really overwhelming," Thomas said. "By noon, the story had gone viral and I started getting calls from the media from all over the globe. It was incredible."[11]

Reinhart and Rogoff did not quite admit their error. Their comment: "We are grateful to Herndon et al. for the careful attention to our original 'Growth in a Time of Debt' paper and for pointing out an important correction to Figure 2 of that paper. It is sobering that such an error slipped into one of our papers despite our best efforts to be consistently careful. We will redouble our efforts to avoid such errors in the future. We do not, however, believe this regrettable slip affects in any significant way the central message of the paper or that in our subsequent work."[12]

Nobel winner Paul Krugman, no fan of austerity, tartly noted that the response was "really disappointing; they're basically evading the critique."[13]

Connectional intelligence provides a framework
for re-examining the past and moving
more confidently into the future.

And Thomas Herndon? It took courage to question what some of the most powerful thinkers in the world had accepted as proven fact. It was dispiriting and disturbing to learn that one of the main tenets of modern economic policy—the idea that slashing government spending is essential to the long-term recovery of struggling economies—simply isn't true. But despite his status as an unknown graduate student, Thomas's work was not lost. He sparked a conversation around the world, and according to Stanford University economist John Taylor, Thomas Herndon's discovery of the error was a factor in easing austerity policy at a 2013 G20 meeting. "It's also a new talking point in the battle over the budget," Taylor noted. "[Thomas Herndon's paper is] offered as a reason why the U.S. should stop worrying about budget reform and consolidation and start worrying about austerity."[14]

We think that as the norms of connectional intelligence spread, this will be one of the by-products: we will re-examine our recent past, what we studied, how we studied and, through the power of connection, discover that ideas and theories we discovered and adopted simply weren't true. We see this story not so much as a "takedown" of previous generations, as some in the media dubbed the David and Goliath story of Thomas Herndon, Reinhart and Rogoff, but as a necessary and thoughtful re-examination of our past that will take us, with confidence, into the future.

WE'RE ALL SURFING THE SAME OCEAN

Fear plays an interesting role in connectional intelligence. We know that innovation is often spurred by fear of necessity, fear of failure and fear of the unknown. Take, for example, the monster waves that we discussed in chapter one. For as long as humans have set sail on the ocean, we've feared big waves—and with good reason. Waves that top sixty, seventy, even eighty feet can and do snap massive cargo vessels in half. But for every sailor who ever feared these waves, there was a surfer who wanted to get closer, who dreamed at night about what it would feel like to be inside the eye of one of these aquatic tornadoes.

Big wave surfing began in the 1930s on the beaches of Waikiki. From the beginning, each advancement in the sport has been a veritable case study in connectional intelligence. The first big wave surfers—John Kelly, Wally Froseith and others in their Waikiki circle—discovered they could ride bigger waves if they did so at an angle, rather than straight down the face. Working together, they changed the shape of the boards they used, carving narrower tails and wider Vs into the boards, which allowed them to navigate larger waves than before. They dubbed these "hot curl boards."[15]

Ten years later, when the original "Riding Giant," George Downing, joined their crew, he refined the technology even more by adding a fin, something he'd spotted during a vacation to Malibu, California. Now, keep in mind that in the 1930s and 1940s big wave surfers were taking on waves of about twelve feet; massive, thrilling, but positively tame by today's standards.[16]

Cut to the modern era, in which Laird Hamilton and his friends—fellow big wave riders Darrick Doener and Buzzy Kerbox—devised a technique that enabled surfers to tackle waves of thirty-five to seventy feet. Working together, they used inflatable boats to tow one another into waves that were too big to catch by the traditional means of paddling in. In a matter of months these three young men pushed surfing further and faster than thousands of avid surfers had done in the hundred years prior. This breakthrough not only changed the face of surfing in Hawaii, but around the world.

Surfing continues to be a hotbed of rapid innovation precisely because connectional intelligence is so embedded into the DNA of its culture. Take Dusty Payne and his group of four buddies, who were determined to put Maui on the surfing map. As we saw in the first chapter, they studied hundreds of hours of videos of themselves and other top surfers, and they didn't stop there. They sought out athletes in adjacent sports around the world—skateboarders, windsurfers, mountain bikers and motor-cross champions. They met with these guys. Filmed them. Talked to them all over the world on Skype. They studied, shot videos, practiced and then practiced more. Dusty invented the "Superman" and went on to win a world junior surfing championship. While Dusty may or may not become "the next Laird Hamilton" of surfing, he has set new standards of excellence and changed the sport again.[17]

Groups of surfers, living in a culture of connectional intelligence, now use technology to communicate globally about the shifting environmental factors of the ocean, to share information about techniques, and to draw wisdom from other extreme athletes—skateboarders, windsurfers, mountain bikers and motor cross champions—to help them learn how to ride the big waves that they love. Surfers understand, intellectually and intuitively, that the ocean they are riding in their corner of the world is connected, literally and figuratively, to the ocean that other surfers are riding all around the world.

GET THERE TOGETHER

Connectional intelligence has always been a natural element of team sports. Even solo sports like tennis rely on a team of experts to help the individual realize and maintain his or her peak performance. But in business, teamwork is not always organic. What we've learned in our work together is that a new form of collaboration in business is one of the strengths of millennials, when used well. They connect because it's one of the things that they know how to do, instinctively and powerfully.

The instinctual power that millennials bring to connectional intelligence can be seen in many fields, but among them, most powerfully, is the old white-shoe law firm. A prestigious New York law firm that pays first-year associates approximately $165,000 may reliably be said to have its pick of a large roster of graduates from distinguished law schools. So it is at Skadden, Arps, Slate, Meagher and Flom, where 1,700 attorneys produce more than $2 billion in fees each year. Those numbers make Skadden one of the more powerful law firms on Wall Street, one of the biggest law firms in the world.

So it was quite a shock, in 2012, when Skadden's CFO noticed that billings were down from a group of associates. It couldn't be that lawyers weren't putting in the hours—there were clients aplenty to keep

attorneys busy. Could it be the associates themselves? No. Senior partners reported that they were an excellent group. Then what was it?

The problem, it turned out, *was* the associates. They were the first
of a new breed. Having grown up in a world where being connected is
the norm, it was natural for them to be collaborators, as well as rivals.
And so they'd created a private network of all the incoming associates,
in which they used a modified version of Twitter to ask each other for
help, advice and information. Got a question? Just ask, and another associate will respond.[18]

Questions emerged on the Twitter network:

- How do I cite this legal document?
- I know we did a similar case in law school, what was the name
  of it?
- Anyone know who I can ask about this type of merger?

Hundreds of shared legal questions, problems and solutions were sent
out. The associates could do this kind of sharing fast, without being distracted from the cases they were working on. This is how they'd always
worked in law school, why change it now?

Yet by following their natural way of working, the associates had
created a quandary for their managers. They were getting more done.
They were doing better work. They felt connected to each other, even
though they knew they were being judged by individual performance.
Sharing made the long hours easier. But they were billing fewer hours.

The old-school solution would have been for the firm to declare
that billing was Skadden's first priority—and to shut down the Twitter
consultations. That's not what happened.

As much as the partners at the top of Skadden may not have liked
change, they understood that this is the future—a better, more powerful system—and that it is natural to the new generation. It was a force

they could not resist. So they decided to learn from the way junior staff was working. They established a Twitter@work program to ensure that all Skadden employees knew that connection with associates was an option. They also launched a reverse mentorship program, assigning a junior associate to each senior law partner, so the associates could teach the partners how to use social software to be more efficient. Yes, the firm's economics changed slightly, but so did its work product—for the better. In the end, Skadden reaffirmed that they win by being the best—it's what really matters. They are just at the beginning of this journey. Thanks to their connectionally intelligent millennials, they are well-equipped to create the future of their profession.

GET THERE FASTER

There is an African proverb that states if you want to go fast, go alone. If you want to go far, go together. While the story of the Skadden first-year associates certainly demonstrates the latter, connectional intelligence is also a useful tool for acceleration. In groups, we can now go faster than we ever imagined.

Take, for example, Mally Roncal, founder of Mally Beauty. A glamorous second-generation Filipino-American, she is known for her shampoo-commercial-perfect hair, her perfectly done eyelashes and what has been called her "happy go-lip-gloss" spirit. When celebrities like Angelina Jolie, Beyonce and Jennifer Lopez want to look their prettiest, they call Mally Roncal. Twenty years in the business has rewarded Mally, now 42, not only with an A-list clientele, but also with a booming beauty empire. She is a regular on QVC, where Mally Beauty has sold more than seven million units. Along with such marquee brands as Perricone MD, WEN Hair Care and Bare Escentuals, Mally Beauty is one of QVC's top five vendors. During her first show on the shopping network, the program—slated for one hour—ended 22 minutes early. QVC had sold out of all the Mally Beauty products they had in stock.[19] As Mally might say, the "Mallynistas" have made her a very wealthy woman.

As an example of American entrepreneurship, her story has very familiar themes. Daughter of hard-working immigrant parents finds her way into a glamorous field, pays her dues and grabs the attention of all the right people. (Did we mention she's also worked with Heidi Klum, Maggie Gyllenhaal and Rihanna?) After building her profile, this entrepreneur opens her own business and is rewarded with resounding success.

Contrast Mally's story with that of twenty-four-year-old Michelle Phan. The daughter of Vietnamese immigrants, Michelle grew up in Sarasota, Florida. She has said, "I never made friends at school; in Florida I was one of the few Asian kids, and I always got made fun of because I was different. To cope, I holed up in my room, drawing superheroes and reading. In one sketch I created a magical version of myself that had the superpower to save my family from our situation."[20] Raised by a single mother, she had no idea how she would pay the $12,000 tuition when she was accepted at Ringling College of Art and Design in Sarasota. Her mother paid the first semester's tuition with money pooled together from aunts and uncles. Michelle promised her mother that the investment in her education would not be lost. She'd find a way to take care of her family, just as her mother had struggled all those years to find a way take care of her and her sisters.

During that first semester, a professor gave each student a MacBook Pro to use in a video design class. Michelle, then eighteen, was attending school during the day and waiting tables at night, to make ends meet. As a hobby, she began creating makeup tutorials on her new MacBook Pro and posting them on YouTube. She not only made videos that showed looks she might wear herself—edgy rocker girl makeup for a night out with friends, sweet pink hues for Sunday church service with her family—she also did more dramatic looks. With the expertise of a skilled film makeup artist, she used drugstore lipsticks and eye shadows, bought on sale and on clearance, to create different characters and personas, just as she had drawn superheroes as a kid.

When she was growing up, as an Asian girl in a predominantly white neighborhood, Michelle had wanted to emulate the white girls around her. "Western beauty is considered the dominant beauty in the world," she said. "Tall, blond, blue eyes. I always felt a little self-conscious because I wanted to be more Caucasian. I tried to get bigger eyes . . . I would dress preppy."[21] But in her videos, Michelle took a different track, creating looks that highlighted and celebrated difference and self-expression. In between her fans' all-time favorites, videos that show you how to get the "Romantic Valentine Look" or "The Mysterious Masquerade Look," Michelle shows looks that are entirely her creation: she has portrayed herself with skin so dark it's almost purple; with a Streisand-inspired profile (when she herself has a button nose), with contacts and fangs and prosthetics. Each look asked the question, "What is beautiful?"[22]

Within months, her YouTube following was so big that she earned more from advertising than she did from her waitressing gig. In 2012, four years after she'd started, with more than two hundred short videos under her belt—all filmed in her bedroom—she earned her first seven-figure paycheck. Michelle's YouTube subscribers began asking her straightforward questions on everything from perfecting black eyeliner to creating a dark complexion, and Michelle shaped her videos based on the input from her community. This interactive dynamic between Michelle and her followers led to the formation of a powerful, growing community that has put her at the forefront of a new way of sharing information. Michelle explains that the members of her community are "the ones steering the ship—they ask the questions, and I create my videos to answer them. Without my followers, I would be working in a void—like a teacher in an empty classroom. Their enthusiasm gives me the motivation and inspiration to educate and share every day."[23]

Google offered her a million dollars to create 20 hours of content. Then L'Oreal came calling, offering Michelle the opportunity to create her own line. Em—named after the Vietnamese word for "little sister" or "sweetie"—made Michelle a millionaire several times over. And she's just getting started. She's accomplished in five years what it took Mally Roncal more than twenty years to do.

Michelle Phan's story matters because it exhibits the power of one young woman driven by passion, working with persistence and using curiosity, community, imagination and intuition—not market research—to make smart business decisions that changed the $170 billion cosmetics industry. If, as a CEO or an executive, you don't think YouTube is something you need to know, study and understand, then consider this: In March 2014, Mac Cosmetics' most-watched video on YouTube was "Viva Glam—Behind the Scenes with Rihanna." The video, for which the company no doubt spent hundreds of thousands of dollars in celebrity endorsement and production fees, has racked up an anemic 58,000 views on the channel. On March 7, 2014, Michelle Phan posted a video called "Matte About You" on her YouTube Channel. In week one, the video had 1.2 million views, which is a standard response from Michelle's fan base. As *Women's Wear Daily* cheekily reported, beauty bloggers like Michelle are "running mascara rings around the major brands."[24]

Michelle Phan showed her connectional intelligence in the way she combines her creativity with the dialogue she keeps up with her fans. In an interview, Michelle said, "I want to empower girls to be daring."[25] There are literally thousands of beauty bloggers, but Michelle has an electric, years-long connection with her fans because she does more than show them how to put on makeup. She connects with an essential need for self-expression, and then gives girls and women both the courage and the step-by-step know-how to be boldly and bravely themselves.

The desire to transform and elevate learning for people is also at the heart of Salman Khan's desire to get big things done. As a boy growing up in Metairie, Louisiana, Khan's family did not have much. But he always knew that he was gifted, especially in math. When he was in the second grade, the teacher asked what each child most liked to do. The seven-year-old told his teacher that he liked to draw and liked puzzles, so she introduced him to Mind Benders—puzzles that challenge deductive thinking. These became the building blocks of what would become Khan Academy. "I learned more in that [second grade] program that applies to what I do today," Salman says, "than in the five other hours of the day combined."[26]

In high school, a wild-haired, ear-pierced Salman played in a death-metal band. He also entered math competitions, regionally and nationally, where his scores allowed him to move from Metairie to Cambridge, Massachusetts. Within four years—"by skipping a lot of classes because there were much more productive ways of learning everything than sitting in lectures"—he got undergraduate and graduate degrees from Harvard and MIT. By 2009, he had a lucrative job in Boston as a hedge fund analyst, an infant son and a wife who was in training for a medical career.

He also had what he called "a hobby."[27]

Salman's young cousin, Nadia, in Louisiana, was having trouble with algebra. To help her, he made some videos and posted them on YouTube. They were unlike any tutorial videos in the world. On the screen, his cousin saw hand-drawn neon-colored equations. Salman did not appear, but his voice narrated each "lesson." For Nadia, and later his other younger cousins, the strength of these videos was that they allowed them to work at their own pace, pausing and reviewing when they didn't understand something, skipping ahead if they were bored.[28]

He saw another advantage of this method: "The very first time you're trying to get your brain around a new concept, the last thing you need is another human being saying, 'Do you understand this?'"

His cousins agreed. Salman says, "They preferred me on YouTube than in person."[29]

Salman made ninety algebra videos, then moved on to geometry, calculus and physics. He imagined that he would become a portfolio manager, have his own fund and "maybe 15 or 20 years in the future, on my own terms, fund a school." The rise in popularity of his educational videos on YouTube, the millions of views and the testimonials of appreciative students prompted him to quit his job, describing the response as the "highest social return that one could ever get." He created a studio in a closet off the bedroom and made more videos. Within a year, 100,000 people were using the videos, online learning was becoming a business, but Khan insisted his videos be free to all. He and his wife agreed that Khan Academy, as it was now called, would have a year to get on its feet financially. If it couldn't make it, he would go back to his old job.[30]

Salman Khan's cousins preferred learning from him on YouTube rather than in person.

Praise poured in, but not dollars. Then the school system in Los Altos, California, which serves 4,500 students, gave him the opportunity to work out a system to "flip the classroom"—lessons would be embedded in the videos and done as homework, while classroom time would be dedicated to more human interactions with teachers and with other students. What happened? Students created peer-action learning groups in the classroom based on their skill level. Teachers began using class time to give individual support to weaker students, while letting stronger students move forward in their learning. And this experience was repeated in classrooms across the country. For example, eighth grade teacher Bryan Harms used Khan Academy data to assess the amount of time spent and the number of topics students focused on, to identify which students needed help and which could provide help, and to diagnose individual strengths and weaknesses.

Building on this, Khan Academy has created a suite of tools for teachers to use while their students are doing work in the classroom. Homework means watching the videos; classroom time is used for the real work of learning—doing the actual work, supported by the tools. Now teachers can see what each student is doing, and get them help where they need it most.

Philanthropists, including Bill Gates, noticed the program's success. Today, in partnerships with the Gates Foundation, Google and many others, Khan Academy offers 5,000 videos in many languages on everything from chemistry to the French Revolution. The Academy not only brings instruction to millions of school students, but to people studying at home, including a growing number of adults with a thirst for learning. Khan's revolutionary motto—"a free world-class education for anyone anywhere"—has become, through his efforts, not just a quixotic pipe dream, but a reality for hundreds of thousands of students all over the world.

> *Khan Academy is a powerful model of inversion that*
> *challenges what we know and teaches us new tricks*
> *with (shoe string) ingenuity and imagination.*

One of the most profound shifts that massive connectivity is creating in education is the shift from what is done in class and what is homework. Khan Academy's system of learning creates an "inversion":

lectures, the traditional method of imparting information and explanations—something done for centuries in the classroom—are now being done by students who watch videos at home, as homework. Working problems and applying the lectures—something traditionally done outside the classroom as homework—is now the center of activity in class by students working individually, in groups and with the teacher. Khan Academy helps teachers see where students are having problems—which allows teachers to then intervene, uncover mental models or other issues driving the mistakes, or clear up misconceptions at the root of the problems. That is, Khan Academy empowers teachers and students to spend their time together in the profound work of developing one another's thinking—at the root of where known concepts meet new imagination and the two combust.

Since we believe that there are as many ways to be connectionally intelligent as there are people, let's pause for a moment and notice each of the connectionally intelligent innovators in this chapter. Take a look at the differences and similarities in the ways that Ron, Dusty, Skadden associates, Michelle and Salman combined people, networks, disciplines and resources, forging connections to create value, meaning and breakthrough results. In Part Three, we'll show you the tools and techniques that these innovators use and how you can use them for yourself.

4

CONNECT INTELLIGENTLY

TOOTH CARE PRODUCTS USED TO BE SOLD IN GLASS JARS, either as powders or as pastes. In 1896, Colgate became the first toothpaste packaged in collapsible tubes. Today, if you ask ten people to name a brand of toothpaste, nine of them would say "Colgate." With good reason—Colgate has been one of America's leading toothpaste brands for more than a century.

Colgate-Palmolive, with 37,400 employees and annual sales of $17 billion, is ranked #64 on the list of World's Most Valuable Brands. It dominates its category: oral care is Colgate-Palmolive's biggest division, and Colgate is the #1 toothpaste brand worldwide. It's the market leader in more than 170 countries.[1]

There are over 200 scientists and researchers at the Colgate Technology Center. It's a large, modern facility designed to inspire creative thinking—Colgate-Palmolive ranks #77 on the list of 2014 Most Innovative Companies. Several years ago, Colgate-Palmolive had a seemingly unsolvable problem. They had come up with a great new formulation for toothpaste with more fluoride, which in turn meant greater efficacy.

They were eager to get the new product to market—from a competitive standpoint, timing mattered. But fluoride is a rather large molecule, and they were having trouble actually packaging the new toothpaste. Because of the chemical flows involved, Colgate's manufacturing plants could not get the new toothpaste into the tubes with the extra fluoride intact. So Colgate put a top R&D team of scientists on the problem. But even that team couldn't fix it right away. "Give us more resources and time, we'll crack the code," they insisted. But they struggled with the basic science needed to meet the challenge.[2]

Faced with a persistent problem that struck at the heart of the company's core business, a top Colgate executive had the courage to ask different questions: What if there is a faster way to solve this? What if there is someone outside Colgate who already knows the answer? What if they would be willing to share the answer with us? How could we find them? What if we asked a crowd of solvers? He convinced his team to partner with an open-source problem-solving site called InnoCentive, on which businesses can present science challenges for which they would welcome outside solutions.

InnoCentive's launch was funded a little more than a decade ago by pharmaceutical giant Eli Lilly as a way to connect with brainpower outside the company—with people who could help develop drugs and speed them to market. Think of it as accelerated corporate R&D, just made up of freelancers. From the outset, InnoCentive opened its doors to allow other firms access to its wide network of specialized experts. Companies like Boeing, DuPont, and Procter & Gamble now post their most challenging scientific problems on InnoCentive's website; anyone on InnoCentive's network can try to solve the problem. The companies generally pay solvers anywhere from $10,000 to $100,000 per solution.[3]

InnoCentive's secret sauce: first, it takes a company's problem, then it "flattens" the problem so it's concise and portable and finally it pushes the challenge out to the world of solvers. Historically, many of the challenges were solved by people whose resumes would not have qualified them to be hired to work on the problem.

Colgate posted its fluoride problem on InnoCentive. Because it was the first time it had presented a challenge for public consumption, its executives had no idea what to expect. As it turned out, they did not have to wait long until one of the freelancers on InnoCentive offered a viable solution.

Ed Melcarek is resourceful and inventive, but after a layoff in mid-career he had a problem he couldn't solve—getting a job. A design engineer and physicist, he'd designed heating vents for buildings and robot arms for spray-painting. But prospective employers weren't impressed by his work history. His skills were "too diverse," they said. He wasn't "a good fit" anywhere he looked.[4]

His savings dwindled. He jokingly considered burning his engineering reference library, throwing away his address book, changing his name, getting a face-lift. Then he discovered InnoCentive, entered an InnoCentive challenge and won an award that, he said, "saved me from the welfare office, and re-affirmed my confidence in myself." Soon he stopped looking for a "regular" job.[5]

As a physicist, Ed Melcarek only had to read the Colgate challenge to realize he had the answer. Really, it was beyond simple: Colgate-Palmolive was approaching the problem from the wrong science—this wasn't a chemistry problem, it was a physics problem. If you put a positive charge on the fluoride paste and grounded the tube, the positively charged particles would flow smoothly into the negatively charged tube, because in physics, opposites attract.

When Ed shot off his solution, light bulbs went on at Colgate-Palmolive. They hired him to do a few hours' work, and then sent him a check for $25,000—a good payday for the engineer, a bargain for the company.

"It's a beautiful way of doing business," he said. Ed now scans the web every week for open innovation challenges. Then he puts on his thinking cap—a floppy fishing hat—and starts to work. His time is valuable, so he commits only a half hour to brainstorming a problem; if he has no answer, he gives up.[6]

Over the years, Ed has won many awards—and plenty of prize money. He's no longer looking for a permanent position. He isn't even looking for consulting gigs: "InnoCentive does all that work with their seeker companies and lets me just do the science." Best of all, he gets to choose which challenges he wants to work on. "I have," Ed says now, "a dream job."[7]

It's the kind of job that appeals to many twenty-somethings as well. Recent studies show that over half of millennials dream of starting their own businesses, and that one in five adults under the age of 34 plans to quit their day job to go solo at some point.[8]

When attracting—and retaining—twenty-something talent is of such a high priority, the lessons of connectional intelligence can help managers lead and mentor young people. Companies that embrace connectional intelligence will attract the best and brightest of the next generation. While connectional intelligence is a human trait, its power is amplified when shared among groups. Organizations can enhance the value of their individual members by building connectional intelligence into the core of their culture. We believe that this will be an essential cultural trait of organizations that survive and thrive in the coming decades. Colgate's experience was transformational. Now Colgate often uses InnoCentive and other open-source problem-solving platforms to share its difficult challenges. It is also rethinking how it connects with its internal scientists, allowing them to opt-in to solve problems (versus working only on what's been assigned to them) and connect across traditional boundaries.[9]

Colgate remains the #1 toothpaste brand worldwide, despite a furious challenge from Crest. Colgate's willingness to go outside its lab and spend $25,000 to look for a solution to a difficult problem? Possibly the best investment the company made that year.

Organizations enhance the value of their people by building connectional intelligence into the core of their culture.

What makes the Colgate story exciting and relevant in our current economic landscape is that it isn't just a story about how big-brain free-lancers can solve tough science problems. Colgate's use of InnoCentive made it a bellwether, and its story shows how we can all be agents of change to help each other supersize our dreams.

Ben Kaufman, the twenty-something founder of Quirky, maintains that twenty-first century product development and manufacturing suffers from a failure to address two problems. One problem is process: changing a cool product *idea* into an *actual* product, available everywhere, is traditionally very hard and slow because of cumbersome financing, engineering, manufacturing, distribution and marketing systems, all deeply entrenched in the way we do business. The second problem is that the manufacturing industry, with its moribund work processes, doesn't welcome or cultivate creative people. As Ben so eloquently puts it, "Practice doesn't make perfect. Passion makes perfect."[10]

Ben hates the turtle-slow pace of development and invention in American manufacturing. Computers may go fast, but the companies that are responsible for creating and making the products that we use in our day-to-day life tend to move really, really slowly. Take for example, this favorite anecdote of Ben's:

Starting in 1930, at the start of the Great Depression, how long did it take to construct the Empire State Building?
One year, a month and twelve days.

How long did it take Lockheed to go from drawing board to fighter jet?
143 days.

And how long did it take a twenty-first century kitchenware company to bring a potato peeler to market?
Three years.

When Ben founded Quirky, he was convinced that there was no shortage of good ideas for products. The problem was that the big companies that manufactured and marketed products only considered ideas from their own employees. If everything new is generated and subjected to internal review, no wonder so many products are slow to get to market.

Ben didn't accept the idea that companies only hire gifted people, or that these people have a monopoly on creativity. He believed that you don't have to be an extraordinary genius, dripping with advanced degrees and a distinguished résumé, to have extraordinary ideas. In the great American populist tradition, Ben believed invention should be universally accessible.

What was missing, he felt, was corporate support for inventors. Bring us ideas, he reasoned, and we'll do the rest. So, he proposed a very twenty-first-century collaboration between a community of online creators and Quirky's in-house product design team.

This collaboration, Ben said, made two previous impossibilities possible: scale and speed. His goal was to launch three products each week. The method he chose is democratic: once a week, he hosts an open Ustream event with his entire staff and the rest of the Quirky community to discuss the week's possible inventions. Led by Ben, the one-hour show is filled with laughter, as he works to get his team members, supplied with beer and wine, to discuss the practicality of making a prototype or the likelihood of someone actually buying it. A sample week's ideas include a "shoelace cutter and crimper, an expandable fiber gift sock wrapping, and a juice carafe that allows users to adjust the level of pulp before pouring." Viewers from home can also vote on whether they like the product and throw in comments via live chat.[11] The creators of the week's best ideas get ten minutes to make their presentations, and then the community votes. Prototypes quickly follow. While Quirky designers create the prototype, they poll the broader community to help them come up with everything from the name, tagline, color, finish and price.

Quirky began with a one-person product development department; there are now hundreds of people on that team. They're needed— Quirky products are sold in 30,000 retail stores. The range of outlets is unusual, from the MoMA design store to Target, Home Depot and Best Buy. Quirky products include everything from electronics, like hip iPhone cases; to kitchen gadgets, like potato peelers; to housewares, like air conditioners.

Then Quirky hit a grand slam home run: a partnership with General Electric (GE).[12] The partnership is literal: GE is sharing its patents and technologies with Quirky's product development team. Why? Because Ben's success with Quirky convinced GE that they wanted access to these kinds of creative products. GE also realized it couldn't afford to wait to do this all on its own. The first projects were in a hot new field: smart, digitally powered technology for the home.[13] Like, for example, an app-enabled milk jug that tells you when the milk is going sour or when you need to buy more.

Ben Kaufman has crowd-sourced his way to a $50 million business. His investors have pumped $97 million into Quirky.[14] All because he built an innovative hybrid based on an engaged global community.

But GE is just icing on the cake. Quirky's biggest achievement is that it has created a universe of partnerships. It has connected every link in the product chain, from inventor to retailer to potential customer. In the process, people who would normally see each other as rivals are innovating together. And of course, for those who dreamed of becoming inventors but never had the time or resources to chase the dream, Quirky has not only created an outlet for innovative design, but also a template for any company that needs to mix a long-established infrastructure with the creativity and digital finesse of the next generation.

Mansuk Prajapati, an Indian entrepreneur and inventor, would be very at home in the world of Quirky. Looking at pictures of smashed earthen pots after a devastating earthquake in his community, Mansuk had an ingenious idea. Villagers often used earthen pots to fetch water and keep it cool. Local newspapers joked that these earthen pots were the "village fridge." Mansuk thought, why not use the earthen clay to make a real fridge, one that looked like a fridge, served the same purpose, but was affordable and didn't require electricity? The result was the Mitticool, India's first non-electric refrigerator. Made of clay and working with existing water systems, the Mitticool allows water from an upper chamber to seep through the sidewalls, cooling the food in the lower chambers through evaporation.[15]

From the start, the Mitticool was a hit in Mansuk's remote Indian village. This dynamic happens all the time: an inventor in a rural and remote place creates something based on a need; it does the job, but never reaches beyond the edge of the village. In the beginning, the Mitticool was no different. Mansuk's neighbors loved it, but he only built them one at a time to sell locally.[16]

Anil Gupta started out as a professor at the Centre for Management in Agriculture at the Indian Institute of Management, Ahmedabad. His job took him to many rural villages where he saw innovations, like the Mitticool refrigerator, that improved the quality of life. He knew more was possible. Walking home from work one day, he saw a honey bee, and it occurred to him that if he could be like the honey bee, life would be wonderful. As Anil tells it, "What the honey bee does: it pollinates, takes nectar from the flower, pollinates another flower, cross-pollinates. And when it takes the nectar, the flowers don't feel shortchanged. In fact, they invite the honey bees through their colors, and the bees don't keep all the honey for themselves."[17]

Anil felt the profound and spiritual pull of his own connectional intelligence. He decided to act. Walking out on his career and his comfortable salary, he founded the Honey Bee Network, which brings together innovators, farmers, scholars, academics, policy makers, entrepreneurs and non-governmental organizations for a cross-pollination of ideas, creativity and practical business advice. The Honey Bee Network acts as a hub, connecting a myriad of agencies to find, source and support grassroots innovations. The goal is to spread the innovations at scale, across India and beyond, to make a difference in the lives of millions.

When the Honey Bee Network found Mansuk, he didn't know that his life was about to change. Although he was intrigued by the idea of selling the Mitticool across India, he realized he faced three challenges. First, he wasn't sure he knew how to manufacture in a way that could meet rising demand. Second, he had no business experience or schooling that would help him create on the commercial scale needed to reach distant markets. The third challenge was himself: he hadn't intended to become a large-scale entrepreneur, and had to decide what he wanted his life to look like.

Through the Honey Bee Network, Mansuk met people who touched and supported his sense of possibility. Over a few months, he realized what he could make possible in the environment of the Honey Bee Network, with all of its—and his—connectional intelligence activated. At first he was surprised at how quickly he could take on new challenges. But even more importantly, he was connected to people who expanded his knowledge, worldview and passion to make a difference. He felt himself grow in ways he could not have imagined. He decided to go for it.

The expertise of the Honey Bee Network, and its comprehensive connections to widespread resources, helped Mansuk protect, patent and scale the Mitticool. This led him to create more user-friendly products out of clay, such as a clay cooker and a clay, non-stick frying pan that retains heat longer than the typical frying pan and retails for only $2 US.

From one man and one idea, a frugal yet fruitful industry has grown, one that employs large numbers of people in his home community and serves thousands of consumers across India and abroad.

It's interesting to note that, unlike Quirky and InnoCentive, the Honey Bee Network is not dependent on fancy, high-speed digital platforms. Of course, as Honey Bee continues to evolve, it will use technology appropriate for the rural communities it serves in any way it can. But Honey Bee's starting point was, and always will be, connecting people, ideas and resources, whether online or off.

It's not just people in developing countries who are connecting to support new sustainable innovation. Nike, along with Best Buy, Creative Commons, IDEO, Mountain Equipment Co-op, nGenera, the Outdoor Industry Association, salesforce.com, 2Degrees and Yahoo! have created an online marketplace, the GreenXchange (GX), in which companies share intellectual property in order to create new environmentally sustainable business models and innovation.[18]

"Nike is committing to placing more than 400 of our patents on GX for research, demonstrating our belief that the best way to stimulate sustainable innovation is through open innovation," said Mark Parker, Nike president and CEO. "Our hope is this will unleash new innovation to help solve current obstacles to sustainability issues."[19]

Noble words. But not words with great appeal to corporate lawyers. In a business environment that worships intellectual property and regards patents as crown jewels, what Nike did was practically heresy. The animus for the idea was to encourage innovation in environmentally sustainable industries in which Nike and the other companies didn't compete. To make such IP sharing more palatable, safeguards were built in: each patent-owner controlled the extent of the patent sharing. For example, when a Nike patent is offered for sharing, any improvements made to that patent must be available to Nike. In that way, Nike both helps the environment by giving green enterprise access to its patents, and, at no additional cost, gets the potential benefit of the creative ideas of hundreds—if not thousands—of scientists, engineers and inventors who extend the use of Nike's patents in the world.

An example of the GreenXchange in action is supplied by the mountain-biking company Mountain Equipment Co-op. The company licensed a Nike environmentally friendly rubber patent to innovate its tire inner tubes, thus bringing a greener product to market more quickly and cheaply than the company could have done on its own.

Another example shows how Nike itself benefits from sustainability efforts: Nike released its Environmental Apparel Design Tool, an online app, based on Nike's Considered Design Index. This tool helps designers everywhere make real-time choices that shape the environmental impact of their wares. The release of the Design Tool was meant to accelerate collaboration between companies, fast track sustainable innovation and decrease the use of natural resources. Cost to Nike to create it: $6 million and seven years of employee effort.

In South Africa, Nike's own designers used the Environmental Apparel Design application to produce football jerseys made from 100 percent recycled polyester. The environmentally clean and technologically smart material used in these jerseys came from plastic bottles—13 million plastic bottles—that were otherwise destined for a landfill.[20]

That was just the beginning. In a single year, as Nike doubled its use of recycled polyester, 82 million plastic bottles were saved from burial in a landfill.[21] Imagine what would happen if every major apparel company used recycled polyester in just a third of its polyester clothes. In that scenario, demand for recycled polyester would top demand for plastic bottles. By putting the tool on the GreenXchange, Nike made it possible to imagine just that.

The GreenXchange challenges other companies to start a connected courageous conversation in which, by sharing their valuable patents, they stand to be rewarded for their commitment to collaboration and their positive societal impact.

In his book, *Where Good Ideas Come From,* Steven Johnson recalls a scene—based on a true story—from a movie many of us remember well, Ron Howard's epic docudrama *Apollo 13.* The spacecraft is damaged by an on-board explosion that cuts off oxygen and electric power to most of the ship. The astronauts move into the lunar module to survive but they are running out of air—they need a "scrubber" to take the carbon dioxide they exhale out of the air. Without a scrubber, they will suffocate, and the lunar module doesn't have a scrubber. The astronauts must improvise.

In the film, Johnson writes, Mission Control creates a "tiger team" of engineers to solve the problem. Deke Slayton, head of flight crew operations, "tosses a jumbled pile of gear on a conference table: hoses, canisters, stowage bags, filters, duct tape and other assorted gadgets—all the gear the astronauts have in the lunar module. 'OK,' he says, 'We have only a few hours to make carbon scrubbers that will clean the air in the lunar module'—and he points to the table—'using only this stuff.'"

It can be even more difficult to transfer life-saving medical technologies developed in the West to indigenous and rural populations elsewhere. José Gómez-Márquez, founder of MIT's Little Devices Lab, believes that local inventors, given the right connection and a little support, can do just what the tiger team did for the astronauts trapped in Apollo 13. That is, with the stuff locally available, they can build "DIY (Do It Yourself) Hacks," creating health technologies that actually work and save lives in their local environments.

"Little," in "Little Devices," means gently funded. Not requiring massive technological support. Capable of being used in Third World environments, where there might be a shortage of pretty much everything.

In the official language:

> The Little Devices Lab at the Massachusetts Institute of Technology explores the design, invention, and policy spaces for DIY (Do It Yourself) health technologies around the world.[22]

Fighting drug-resistant tuberculosis in developing countries where electricity is scarce and unreliable is a hard problem. The only known effective drug requires patients to take several doses per day for eighteen months. And this drug is temperature-sensitive—it can't be exposed to serious heat or cold. How could the drug be stored safely without a reliable source of electricity?

The MIT Little Devices Lab, working with African engineers and the limited materials available to locals, devised a cooler called "CoolComply" that can run on either electric power or solar cells. The cooler has built-in circuitry that monitors the container's temperature and generates an alarm if it rises too high. To track whether patients are taking their medicine when they should, each cooler records the date and time every time it's opened and a single dose packet is dispensed. This information is then sent via a built-in cell phone to a central health facility.

The alternative? Daily ice deliveries that would cost $600 a year—twice as much as the CoolComply system.

Prototype devices have been field-tested in Addis Ababa, Ethiopia. Users may welcome them. Local engineers already have. "This is something I can actually see being used by people I know," one African engineer said of the cooler. Looking at an MRI machine in the local hospital, he remarked, "Nobody I know will ever use this."[23]

José Gómez-Márquez sees possibility where others don't. "A toy today is really an engineered device. Toys have a much better supply chain than other devices. Plastic toys are everywhere, even at open-air markets in remote towns."[24] He encourages health care workers to take them apart to harvest the parts.

One of the Little Devices Lab's iconic success stories is its collaboration with Yamilet Mendoza Martínez, a nurse at the Hospital Escuela Regional Santiago Jinotepe-Carazo in Jinotepe, Nicaragua. It was inefficient for busy, overtaxed nurses to keep popping into a patient's room to see if a bag of IV fluid needed to be changed. If only an alarm could be attached to the bag . . . In a toy store, she spotted a toy AK-47 that buzzed when fired. She bought it, and attached the toy gun to an IV pole with a clothespin. As the IV bag emptied, a rubber band opened one side of the clothespin, putting it in contact with the gun's trigger. When the bag was empty, the gun buzzed. This "hack" saved lives. Without the connection to the Little Devices Lab, Yamilet would not have known where to start. The connection went both ways. The Little Devices Lab learned from Yamilet, and spread her awesome DIY Hack around the world, for others to use or emulate.[25]

In advertising, the bragging rights to one of the greatest DIY hacks belongs to a thirty-eight-year-old advertising exec named Bonin Bough. His hack began with curiosity about a phenomenon industry people were calling "The Second Screen." More and more consumers were watching TV with their iPads in their laps and their iPhones in their hands. They tweeted one another during sports events, checked players' touchdown or batting stats online and posted real-time game updates on Facebook, Twitter and elsewhere. Bough knew he was guilty of the same behavior. His insight: why not target consumers where they are while they're at it?[26]

The Super Bowl is the biggest televised event in the United States. Watched by 125 million people, it's Christmas and New Year's and Oscar night rolled into one. Advertisers pay for the privilege: in recent years, the average cost of a 30-second commercial was around $4 million.[27]

Bonin decided to test his "Second Screen" theory at Super Bowl XLVII in 2013. It was the ultimate "go big or go home" moment. If it went horribly wrong, Bonin, the global vice president of consumer engagement at Mondelez, could have lost his job.

Oreo cookies, a Mondelez brand, was a sponsor of Super Bowl XLVII. For the game, Bonin assembled an "Oreo team" that included a company lawyer, a marketing executive and the digital marketing agency 360i, with the goal of creating real-time content, relevant to what was happening on the field.

The football game could have been boring, but luckily, it wasn't. There was an unforeseen circumstance: a twenty-two-minute blackout during the third quarter that stopped the game for thirty-four min-utes.[28] As electricians and engineers scrambled to restore electrical power at the stadium, another group of professionals was also working against the clock.

"We had a mission control set up at our office with the brand team and 360i, and when the blackout happened, we looked at it as an oppor-tunity," agency president Sarah Hofstetter explained. "Because the brand team was there, it was easy to get approvals and get it up in minutes."[29]

What they came up with was 140 characters for Twitter. "Power out? No problem. You can still dunk in the dark." The image showed a dark background, a circle of light and one Oreo.

It was a much simpler concept than the $4 million Oreo ad that had run, just minutes earlier, during half time. And at least a thousand times more effective. Within minutes, the Oreo blast was retweeted more than 14,000 times and Oreo's Facebook page had received more than 20,000 likes. All told, it attracted 525 million media impressions. And the Tweeted ad, which cost the team just a fraction of what it might spend on a regular campaign, went on to win a Silver Lion for Digital Marketing from Cannes Lion, Clio awards for Social Media and Innovative Media and an *Adweek* Project Isaac award. The ad established Bough as one of the most connectionally intelligent executives of his generation.[30]

From the Super Bowl to the World Cup, creating real-time creative content, timed to what's happening on the field, is more difficult than it seems.

Bonin Bough scored so big with Oreo that in the months after the Super Bowl, dozens of ad execs tried to recreate his particular blend of real-time marketing magic, but such on-the-spot brilliance is more difficult than it seems. In 2014, the Dutch airline KLM went for what they hoped would be "their Oreo win." After Mexico lost to the Netherlands' in the quarter-finals of the 2014 World Cup, KLM sent out a tweet with a drawing of a sombrero and a giant mustache next to its Departures sign. The tweet read "Adios Amigos! #NEDMEX."[31]

So many things went wrong, so quickly, that it was almost painful to watch the blowback. First of all, for soccer fans around the world, the outcome of the match had been hotly contested, as the Netherlands' win depended on what many fans believed was a poor penalty call by the ref. But more importantly, KLM, which has a big Mexico City hub, offended hundreds of thousands of potential customers by using what many consider outdated, if not offensive, imagery. The noted Mexican actor and director Gael Garcia Bernal tweeted back: "@KLM I'm never flying your sh**ty airline again. F*** you big time."[32] The barrage of tweets the airline received, as well as the hundreds of articles that painted the tweet as the "anti-Oreo," was proof that KLM not only got it wrong, they got it *really* wrong. Although the airline promptly removed the tweet, it is now associated as closely with the 2014 World Cup as Bonin Bough's brilliant Oreo ad is associated with the 2013 Super Bowl.

5

COURAGE BUILDS
ON COURAGE

CONNECTIONAL INTELLIGENCE ISN'T JUST ABOUT WINNING big in business or pursuing an ambitious creative dream. More and more, people are using technology and connectional intelligence to respond within minutes and hours to natural disasters, political uprisings and terrorist acts and to other human suffering, from a neighbor in trouble to an anonymous text from a teen in anguish. Courage feeds on courage. This is one way connectional intelligence really goes big. Something you read in this book could help you tap into your own connectional intelligence when calamity strikes.

Connectional intelligence isn't just about winning big in business. People are using it to respond within minutes and hours to natural disasters and crisis situations.

Kenya was torn apart by widespread violence following a contested presidential election at the end of 2007. Mass protests, murderous rampages and rapes were met by police shootings. No one was safe.

As Ory Okolloh has explained it, "Africa is a complex continent full of contradictions."[1] As part of a new generation of African leaders, who grew up with both the pride and history of her nation and the connectional intelligence of her time, she knew those contradictions well. Ory Okolloh was born in Kenya in 1977, a tumultuous time in the continent's history.[2] It was the year that the death of Steven Biko, the legendary anti-apartheid activist in South Africa, ignited the movement that would topple the entire system. When Ory was three years old, neighboring Uganda suffered one of the worst famines in history: 21 percent of the population died, and 60 percent of infants never lived to see their first birthday.[3] It was in this context that Ory's parents, who were barely scraping by themselves, conspired to divert every available resource toward her education.

Although she made dozens of visits to the principal's office in her Nairobi private school and was threatened with expulsion because her parents were late with her school fees, she—and they—persevered. She earned scholarships to the University of Pittsburgh and then to Harvard Law School.[4] Ory had escaped and excelled. But when the widespread violence erupted in Kenya in 2007, she faced the defining moment of her young life. When you are lucky enough to do well and rise above, what do you owe those you have left behind?

Ory became part of a team that launched Ushahidi.com, a network that uses a mixture of text messages and Google Maps to help Kenyans report what they see happening. Ushahidi is the Swahili word for "testimony." In a country with many more cell phones than computers, these eyewitness accounts of murders, rapes and massacres mostly came in by phone texts—and were largely read there. Soon the site had 45,000 users, and its founders realized they had a base from which they could form a nonprofit tech company, specializing in developing free, open-source software.[5]

The platform created by Ushahidi.com would become valuable again on a hot and humid afternoon in January 2010, when a catastrophic earthquake struck the island of Haiti. Many buildings collapsed, leaving hundreds of thousands of people trapped, wounded, or dead in the dust and debris. A massive rescue and recovery effort followed. But Haitians and disaster relief teams lacked reliable information. Reports were coming in piecemeal; rumors abounded. And huge aftershocks were still happening. Where were the survivors? What condition were they in? How many were dead? Who had water? What medical care was most urgently needed?

Patrick Meier, who grew up in Kenya and had been part of the first Ushahidi mapping operation there, was now a graduate student at Tufts University in Massachusetts and co-founder and co-director of the Harvard Humanitarian Initiative's Program on Crisis Mapping and Early Warning. Within an hour of the earthquake, he saw press reports suggesting that the quake may have killed 100,000 people. Worried about friends working in Port-au-Prince, he did what he had done before: he made a map, put it on Ushahidi.com and tweeted his friends, asking for their location and status.[6]

In the years since its inaugural effort in Kenya, Ushahidi's technology had improved such that it was now able to record every form of input, whether it originated from a cell phone, YouTube, e-mail or a tweet. As in most poor countries, the people of Haiti were not likely to own computers, but many did have cell phones, or knew someone who did. So it didn't take long for Patrick Meier to get a reassuring response from several of his friends—and to see that the enormity of the catastrophe would require many more hands.

The first challenge Patrick addressed was to make the Haitian map as accurate as possible. Using satellite imagery he received from the

World Bank, he mobilized hundreds of volunteers to quickly create the most detailed road map of Haiti ever produced. Working from Boston, Patrick and his team of Ushahidi volunteers were able to provide GPS coordinates for seven key locations in which Haitians were known to be trapped under rubble.

Every piece of information he received from sources in Haiti and around the world went on the map, which was continually updated and available round the clock. To expand Ushahidi's reach, Patrick put out a call on his Twitter feed for a toll-free tracking number that would allow Haitians to get in touch. Someone in Cameroon saw the tweet and connected Patrick with a colleague who worked at the largest telecommunications company in Haiti.

Cell towers were among the first repairs on the ground; within days, the tracking number was up and running, broadcast on social media and by radio stations as the piecemeal power restoration got them back on the air. One of the earliest tweets received came from a woman named Regine in Port-au-Prince, announcing the name and location of a pharmacy that was open, where people could *acheter des medicaments*—buy medicine. Onto the map went the pharmacy address at Rue Lamarre.

Language was the next problem, as much of the information pouring in from Haiti was in Creole. Translation software was inadequate and time-consuming; the group needed human translators. Patrick put out a call on Facebook, and Haitian-born volunteers near Boston poured into the makeshift situation room, providing not only instant language help but native knowledge of the country that was immeasurably useful to the whole operation.

Yet the need was still growing. Patrick began training more volunteers to monitor social and mainstream media for relevant content. Soon there were 100 graduate and undergraduate students—"digital humanitarians"—monitoring media 24/7 for relevant content. Twenty-five days after the earthquake, Ushahidi-Haiti had mapped about 2,500 reports.[7]

The ultimate assessment of this effort came from a spokesman for the United States Marines:

> Your site saved lives. . . . The Marine Corps is using your project every second of the day to get aid and assistance to the people that need it most. . . . YOUR data and YOUR work is putting aid and assistance directly on the target and saving lives. . . .
>
> Keep up the good work!! You are making the biggest difference of anything I have seen out there in the open source.[8]

In Kenya, Ushahidi.com was the superior source for those reporting violence in (almost) real time as well as collecting information from rural areas; later, it was used for raising relief funds from abroad. Connectionally intelligent humanitarians have used Ushahidi.com wherever there was a need for both cutting-edge technology and humanistic data gathering. The platform was used to map violence in eastern Congo, monitor elections in Mexico and India and collect eyewitness reports during the 2008–2009 Gaza war. What Ory Okolloh and her expat twenty-something friends created, using both their heads and their hearts, was also an invaluable data and mapping tool after the Chilean earthquake of 2010, the 2014 winter storms in North America and the wildfires in Russia.

What makes the Ushahidi.com platform so powerful is that it can integrate information sent by anyone connected by almost any means. Add to Ushahidi.com, the connectional intelligence of people like Patrick Meier, and we see how combining disparate individuals, groups and information can and does indeed save lives. Courage builds on courage. This way of combining and forging connections is becoming a go-to template for crisis management around the world.

Ushahidi bills itself, rightly, as the fire hose of global data. But sometimes you don't need a fire hose. There are times when going small, with focused connectional intelligence, is the way to get big things done.

In 2011, the city of Cairo was on fire. Protesters gathered in Cairo's Tahrir Square. Security forces mobilized. Tear gas, beatings and the use of guns firing real ammunition soon followed.

Ahmed Abulhassan, then twenty-three, a former Cairo resident now living in Dubai, watched the scene on his television and realized that many of his friends were in Tahrir Square. From his vantage point, he could see that there was inadequate communication between the activists helping the wounded and the tent hospitals set up a few blocks away. Although his academic degree was in pharmacy biotechnology, like most young graduates he'd also mastered new forms of connection. In addition to the television, he began to engage many other screens: YouTube video clips, Twitter stream, phone, BlackBerry messenger, Skype, e-mails, Google Talk and WhatsApp.

Ahmed felt left out of the relief efforts because he was an Egyptian living abroad. But he couldn't shake the feeling that he wasn't as powerless as he felt. "I kept looking at my Twitter timeline and I saw, hidden between every twenty or so tweets, a call for help," he said. "Some asked for medicines, some asked for surgical tools, and in the middle of all the panic, they probably were not going to be seen. So, on Monday the 21st I started @TahrirSupplies."[9]

His technique was both simple and masterful. From the tweets on his Twitter timeline, he collected a list of supplies needed, removed excess wording in the message to make it more clear, then re-posted it via the @TahrirSupplies account, once in Arabic and once in English. He wanted people to follow an account dedicated to communicating messages about what was missing in the field hospitals so he used a clear, bold, red avatar to stand out. Followers of @TahrirSupplies increased by the hundreds every hour. By the time the Twitter handle had been up twenty-four hours, it had well over 10,000 followers.[10]

Ahmed defined the mission of the humanitarian Twitter handle concisely so that everyone understood: "Our role was to simply communicate a message from the field hospitals to the people. This did not need any ground presence. We would basically stay up for the full 24 hours and make full use of every single technological tool we could think of to keep us in touch with anyone who wanted to make a request. So we were available on Twitter, phone, BBM, Skype, e-mails, Google Talk and WhatsApp all through the day and night."[11]

The Twitter messages were stripped-down communications, telegraphs of pure need in 140 characters or less:

They need more PRISOLINE eyedrops in TAHRIR

NOW blood is needed in[sic] ElDemerdash, ElHelal, ElMonira & Ahmed Maher hospitals

If u wnt 2 send supplies 2 Tahrir tmrw drop them off at Euro Deli

Hospital in central garden needs juices

Main hospital confirmed they need nothing now but cold medicines (anything)

Doctor is urgently needed for a man shot in the chest in Kasr ElEiny Elfransawy[12]

To get the word out, Ahmed reached out to various Egyptian celebrities and popular Twitter users—people with hundreds of thousands of followers—and asked them to retweet him. By managing hundreds of texts and phone calls and tweets, he could learn which hospitals had which needs, then turn around and tweet that information. Doctors could find out where they were needed, and Egyptian citizens could hurry to the nearest pharmacy, buy supplies and send them to the right place. Ahmed, with no experience as a coordinator, had developed a highly collaborative real-time aid organization.[13]

Over a six-day period, coordination needs got bigger. Three Egyptian women in their early twenties offered to help, although none of them were physically present in Tahrir Square. One lived in England, and two lived in Cairo but had parents who did not allow them to join the street action. Over four days, the group slept in rotation and took turns managing Twitter requests 24/7. Soon the requests were so numerous that they needed to set up a Google Docs spreadsheet to track the array of necessary goods, items like Hemostop to seal wounds and Ventolin spray to heal lungs scarred by tear gas. The most dramatic request: an eye surgery machine for anesthetizing eyes. Each machine cost $20,000. In five hours, @Tahrir Supplies mobilized wealthy Cairo residents who gave enough money to buy two machines. Another remarkable outcome: within a week, the tent hospitals received supplies worth about $1 million.[14]

Later in this book, we'll talk about a phenomenon that cultural psychologists call "uncovering"—basically, removing the mask that we all sometimes wear and connecting with the power of our authentic selves. Creating @TahrirSupplies helped Ahmed uncover several powerful things about himself. He discovered his power to use connections, to respond and make a profound difference to thousands of people caught in a violent crisis of national proportions. This changed the way he understood himself and his place in the world. And it super-sized what he now knows can be possible in others.

Connectional intelligence gives us new eyes from which to see others—imagining new possibilities in everyone we meet.

This story illuminates how we can press past our perceived limits: distance, culture, family and political boundaries, to help people in need. The demonstrations uncovered Ahmed's misgivings about being an expat, living far away from the conflict. Through his critical work at @TahrirSupplies, he not only made peace with where he was in his life, he realized that his connectional intelligence allowed him to create a role that felt right for him and deepened his ties to his homeland. Cultivating connectional intelligence not only develops a tool for action and accomplishment, it grounds us in who we are, reminds us of what is important and helps us strengthen the ties that nourish us, emotionally and intellectually. Connectional intelligence gives us new eyes through which to see others—to imagine new possibilities in everyone we meet.

Note that Ahmed didn't post any personal thoughts about politics. He could have. "People were asking, 'What's your message?'" he said. He had no message. He was just trying to do one job: get medical supplies to people in need, no matter which side of the conflict they were on. Twitter can be polarizing, and thinking out loud in the digital world can get you into a lot of trouble, but Ahmed was able to mobilize intergenerationally and across political lines because he kept his eyes on the prize of the greater humanitarian good: @TahrirSupplies was about saving lives and helping people, period.

Courage builds on courage. When we tap into our connectional intelligence, even under duress and devastating conditions, we can connect to powerful solutions that heal and that transform the chaos around us.

Shiza Shahid was a recent Stanford grad and first-year McKinsey consultant when she heard about the terrible shooting of a girl she knew, a girl who had inspired her own work and sense of purpose: Malala Yousafzai, a teenage education rights activist, who had long campaigned for girls' schooling.

Shiza was an undergraduate at Stanford when she first met Malala at a summer camp that she and other students had organized for thirty young Pakistani girls. As Shiza explained, "The camp gave the girls a break from the chaos of their daily lives—the Taliban was actively shutting down schools for girls at the time—and the chance to learn to be activists, both for themselves and for their communities."[15]

When she was only eleven, Malala had begun writing a blog for the BBC. Using a pseudonym, she detailed the effects of the Taliban's refusal to allow girls to attend school and promoted her desire for an education, not just for herself but for all the girls she knew. Newspapers declared her "the most famous teenager in the world," and the South African bishop and activist Desmond Tutu nominated her for the International Children's Peace Prize. From the depths of Pakistan's Swat Valley, in a time and place in which girls had no voice, Malala was being seen, heard and heralded. Then one day, when she was just fifteen years old, a Taliban gunman stopped the school bus in which she was riding, asked the driver to point to Malala and fired three times. One bullet traveled through her head, damaging the left portion of her brain and lodging in her shoulder. Six days after her treatment in Pakistan she was transferred to a hospital in London for further care. Shiza Shahid had been on business in Cairo, but she took the first available flight to London to see her old friend.[16]

Now, just a few years after the two met, she sat by Malala's bedside, not knowing if her friend would live. One of the first things that Malala said when she woke up was that she wanted to continue her campaign. The media was swarming, donations were pouring in, but Shiza saw through the noise of what could easily have become an uneasy martyr-like status for her fifteen-year-old friend and realized that the moment could be used to build a sustainable model of activism. Or as she put it, "How do we leverage her voice in a way that drives all this energy around Malala into meaningful action?" It was at that moment, with twenty-two-year-old Shiza at the helm, that the Malala Fund was born.[17]

The task these young women have set for themselves is nothing short of monumental. The Malala Fund hopes to reach out to girls all over the world, as they eloquently explain: "There are 600 million girls in the developing world. They are an undeniable force for social and economic impact. But only if given the opportunity. Around the world, girls are denied a formal education because of social, economic, legal and political factors. And in being denied an education, society loses one of its greatest and most powerful resources. The Malala Fund aims to change that."[18] While it is just getting started, Malala's message is already being celebrated around the world. In 2014, at the age of 17, she was awarded the Nobel Peace Prize for her work championing the rights of all children to an education. She is the youngest person ever to receive this prize.

Sometimes the call for help is quieter and for a time gets lost in the noise of online conversation. DoSomething.org was started more than twenty years ago by actor Andrew Shue (then a teen heartthrob on the popular show, *Melrose Place*) and his best friend from childhood, Michael Sanchez. Their goal when they launched was simple: inspire and enable young people, twenty-five and under, to take action locally and nationally about the issues they care about. The organization has been a resounding success. DoSomething.org now has 2.7 million members, and the campaigns it has helped launch have taken on everything from homelessness, to bullying, to sexual assault.[19]

Four years ago, Nancy Lublin, who described herself as the "CEO and Chief Old Person"[20] of DoSomething.org, saw a declining response to e-mail campaigns. At the same time she saw that, for teens, texting was "eleven times more powerful than e-mail"—the "open rate" of texts was 100 percent.[21] Your kid may not have answered your text about what time she would be home, she noted, but you can be sure that she read it.

As DoSomething.org moved from e-mail to texting as its primary platform, Nancy began to notice that teens weren't just reading the texts the organization sent, they were texting back, sometimes about the troubles in their own lives:

I was cutting, my parents found out, and so I stopped. But I just started again an hour ago.

I'm afraid to go to school today. The boys call me faggot.

Nancy will never forget a text from a girl who wrote, "He won't stop raping me. He told me not to tell anyone. It's my dad. Are you there?"[22]

As she sifted through the texts and tried to get teens the help they needed, Nancy knew that what she was seeing was a crisis wave that her team was not equipped to address. To meet the needs, DoSomething .org had to completely rethink its mission and the role it played in teen's lives.

Although the intervention was not what DoSomething.org had been built for, Nancy and her team decided to put their collective expertise and technological know-how together to address the troubled side of teenage life with a Crisis Text Line. Partnering with six crisis centers across the country that offered expert counseling on the issues most troubling to adolescents—suicide, depression and sexual abuse—the Crisis Text Line exchanged nearly a million texts with 9,000 teenagers in the first six months after its 2013 launch.[23]

The difference between this crisis line and the phone services that have been around for decades? For teens, a phone call is public—it can be overheard. As anyone who's interacted with teens knows, it can be hard to get words out of them in person. Via text, they can speak as openly and eloquently as they want. Texting, although permanently recorded in a way that phone calls rarely are, feels private and unremarkable to teens. Equally useful, said Nancy, is the electronic record left by conversations via text. When a phone call is over, it's over, but the whole digital history of a text exchange shows up every time contact is made. This record of texts may be useful to an adolescent when there's another crisis and critical when it comes to formulating social policy. Texting has opened a new door on a scope of problems from physical abuse to mental and emotional health issues that were, at a different time, dealt with individually by different agencies.

Think of the old model of the after-school special. From 1972 to 1997, ABC ran dramatic, sometimes controversial, TV shows about issues that faced young people. The after-school specials ranged in topic from illiteracy to anorexia, from substance abuse to teenage pregnancy. Each script was steeped in research on one particular topic, each episode's producer coordinated with help lines and experts from the nonprofit or government agency tasked with handling that particular problem.

The lessons for DoSomething.org were of monumental importance. There was no room for cross-pollination, and no way to address the way issues overlapped. If a teen who had bulimia was also being bullied, the after-school special and its outreach was only designed to handle one of those problems at a time. Or if a teenage boy was struggling with his sexuality and also had a drinking problem, he'd have to call two separate help lines. Can you imagine? The difference between asking a teen to call multiple help lines versus responding holistically to the text he or she has sent is a sea change in how we hear and respond to the challenges and crisis of teenagers, some of our most fragile citizens.

Until now, Nancy says, there has been "no census"—that is, no real-time data—on teens and their troubles. Now she can tell you that the issues young people care most about are animal abuse and homelessness, "because they can see it." Her team knows that children with eating disorders seek help most between Sunday and Tuesday. Self-cutters do not wait until after school to hurt themselves. Depression among teens in El Paso, Texas is three times as high as it is for the same group in Chicago, Illinois. Armed with findings like this, Crisis Text Line recently launched Crisis Trends and published its first set of data online. Now journalists, researchers and concerned citizens can access its findings—which break down the occurrence of specific teen crises by time of day, day of week, over time and by state—and become part of a connected force in the fight to keep teens safe. Nancy and her team are also now coordinating with local governments, school principals, local mental health clinics, data experts and parent groups to influence public policy shaping teens.[24]

The Crisis Text Line has redefined what it means to care, to make a difference and to help teens and their communities, by connecting and interweaving a wide cadre of expertise, relationships and data.

In many stories, including this one, we've seen that connectional intelligence is something that you use to get big things done. But, sometimes, connectional intelligence first requires that you be open, able to see the shifting landscape that's presented to you. And second, it often requires you to rethink your role and to reconfigure your connections to individuals, groups and crowds, to answer emergent needs.

Connectional intelligence is a force that can be used
for so much good, but the force itself is agnostic.

This was certainly the case of Nancy Lublin and DoSomething .org. It was not hyperbole for Nancy to say that DoSomething.org's crisis line might have saved "more lives than penicillin."[25] Penicillin is credited with saving more than 100 million lives in the twentieth century. With DoSomething.org's Crisis Text Line exchanging over 3.4 million messages with teens each year, who knows how many lives might be saved? The metrics for influence and change are nothing short of remarkable.[26]

Connectional intelligence is a force that can be used for so much good, but the force itself is agnostic. Sometimes in the quest to get big things done, people take shortcuts that not only cross the boundary between right and wrong, but dishearten and dispirit the people they once inspired and engaged. It's a story that, by now, many of us know well.

Bicyclist Lance Armstrong had testicular cancer that spread to his brain, lungs and stomach. His chance of surviving surgery and chemotherapy was less than 50 percent, but he not only beat his disease, he went on to win the Tour de France seven times. He started a charity called "Livestrong," and millions of fans not only donated money but wore his campaign's yellow wristband. His endorsement fees became astronomical.[27]

Surely, a man so prominent and visible would never risk his reputation and hard-won health with injections acquired on the black market. He didn't need that—he was a global hero. A god. And gods don't cheat.

But bicycle racing has, historically, been notorious for cheating, and Lance Armstrong was not an exception. He injected Erythropoietin, or EPO, which boosts red blood cell production and increases oxygen, crucial to a rider on the tortuous hills of the Tour de France. He not only used EPO, he encouraged teammates to use it and received treatments in their presence. And he got away with it—no one wanted to cross Lance Armstrong. He was that powerful.

Armstrong—handsome, quotable, promotable—was a great story. Reporters told the story his way. In a business where access matters a great deal, the press tended not to challenge him. And when they did, he sued and won—as when his case against *The Sunday Times* of London resulted in a £300,000 settlement.[28]

There was no chink in his personality, no spark of conscience that might burst into flame and cause him to blurt out the truth about his blood doping. He even turned the rumors of his cheating into positive publicity, as in a Nike commercial in which he said, "Everybody wants to know what I'm on." His answer? On his bike six hours a day. And then he confronted the viewer, asking, "What are you on?"

So how was he brought down?

By the connectional intelligence of a ragtag fraternity of former associates, a group of scientists who had never met him and a handful of determined bloggers.

Let's start with Emma O'Reilly, a young Irish woman who had been Armstrong's assistant. In the book *L.A. Confidential,* she opened up about "transporting doping material across borders, disposing of drugs and syringes when the authorities were lurking, and distributing performance-enhancing substances to the team's riders whenever they needed them." Why did she speak out? "By not saying anything, you're part of the problem," she said.[29] To Armstrong, *she* was the problem—he sued her for libel. Although the case was eventually settled out of court, it severely damaged Emma's reputation and took a heavy emotional toll.[30]

Then there was Betsy Andreu, wife of Frankie Andreu, Armstrong's former teammate. She'd been on the inside. She'd seen the blood doping. And she'd seen what happened when her husband declined Armstrong's invitation to join the party—he was forced off the team.[31]

Armstrong believed that Betsy, like everyone else in his inner circle, would continue to enable his cheating. To his surprise, she wouldn't. "I didn't decide to take Lance on," she explained. "I decided not to lie for him; there's a difference."[32] With that, she said, Armstrong launched Plan B, publicly questioning her sanity and sullying her character.

"I was painted as bitter, jealous, vindictive," she said. "Reporters would use those words, and I wouldn't be called for a rebuttal. Then, down in the comments section, readers would just be going off on me. And the people who employed Frankie would see it, and it would reflect badly on him. The sentiment from the teams that hired him was, 'This publicity is not good for the sport. Why can't she just be quiet?'"[33]

The turning point was a blog, NYVelocity.com, founded in 2004 by Andy Shen—an amateur racer, though not a journalist—and his

friends, Alex Ostroy and Dan Schmalz. They featured the full tran-
script of an interview with Floyd Landis, a disgraced cyclist who claimed
Armstrong had initiated a doping program for his team. And then they
published a technically detailed, 13,000-word interview with a group of
scientists, led by Dr. Michael Ashenden, about Armstrong's drug tests
in which Armstrong's methods were described as the most complicated
doping scheme the scientists had ever seen. The experts showed scientific evidence that clearly indicated doping, throughout the last decade
of Armstrong's biking history.[34]

Social media buzz began to grow, fed by NYVelocity.com's evidence that Armstrong's success was attributed to his use of EPO, an
oxygen-enhancing hormone, and many other drugs. Twitter critics @
TheRaceRadio, @UCI_Overlord and @FestinaGirl joined NYVelocity
.com's blog team and openly shared their suspicions that Armstrong's
success was due to the effectiveness of EPO. NYVelocity.com became
a clearinghouse for the truth, as new evidence emerged and drug tests
proved the use of EPO in Armstrong's samples.[35] The debate on social
media persisted, but mainstream journalists ignored the claims.

A fundamental principle of democracy is free speech, in which
citizens and the press hold people accountable for the truth. From this
perspective, the bloggers, scientists and citizens who brought down
Armstrong were defenders of the democratic system. One important
function of connectional intelligence is to collectively search for, and
protect, truth.

As for Armstrong himself, he continues to wrestle with his disgrace
in private.[36] He lost all of his endorsements and much of his ill-gotten
wealth, and, at the time this book was published, was still in the midst
of settling lawsuits against him for millions of dollars.[37] But he also
continued to be a beacon for cancer victims. There were rumors that
the Livestrong organization wanted him back in the fray. As one of his
friends put it, "Lance was a motherf***er for cancer."[38] Eight million

people die of cancer every year. If Lance Armstrong, with all of his faults—arrogance, greed, duplicity—can get big things done in the world of cancer research, and can serve as a living symbol of how an impossible diagnosis does not have to be a death sentence, perhaps he deserves another chance.

Everyone agrees that it wasn't arrogance that brought down Somaly Mam. Mam is a Cambodian activist, who, until 2014 headed the Somaly Mam foundation, an organization that bravely saved the lives of thousands of young girls who were being sold into sex trafficking. Her fans were some of the most powerful men and women in American public life, including former Secretary of State Hillary Clinton, actress Susan Sarandon and Pulitzer Prize–winning *New York Times* journalist Nicholas Kristof. All of them had visited Cambodia with Mam, toured the shelters and refugee centers that she founded and operated.[39]

Mam herself claimed to have been abducted by a sex trafficking brothel at the age of nine. In an interview at *Fortune*'s Most Powerful Women Summit, she told Facebook's Sheryl Sandberg, "I have been sold in the brothel by the man who come and tell me that he's my grandfather," she said. "I stayed in the brothel nearly ten years. The brothel owner bring us all together, we all sit on the ground, and he tell us we have to do what he ask us to do. But one girl . . . she refused to do what he asked to do so he take a gun and kill her, so that is the day that I have been escaped from the brothel."[40]

She had endured so much, yet instead of settling into the comfortable life she eventually created for herself in France, Mam continued to return to Phnom Penh because her life, as she so often told the media, was with "my girls."

In 2014, some of the most high-profile girls, girls who had appeared on television and in documentaries with Mam, began to cave. Allegations, that were soon substantiated, began to emerge that Mam had given sex trafficking "backstories" to some of the girls who had come to her refugee camp for an education or a shot at a better life.[41] But even before the *Newsweek* cover that would be her downfall, writers and bloggers were beginning to notice that Mam was also having trouble keeping her own story straight. As Simon Marks wrote in his searing *Newsweek* cover story on Mam:

> In February 2012, while speaking at the White House, she said she was sold into slavery at age 9 or 10 and spent a decade inside a brothel. On The *Tyra Banks Show*, she said it was four or five years in the brothel. Her book says she was trafficked when she was "about 16 years old."
>
> Mam's confusion isn't limited to her book, or the backstory for some of "her girls." In 2012, she admitted—after being confronted with some of my early reporting—that she had made false claims in a speech to the UN General Assembly in which she said eight girls she had rescued from the sex industry were killed by the Cambodian army after a raid on her shelter in 2004.[42]

The exposure of Mam's story didn't just shame her, it has caused fundraisers—particularly those who fundraise on behalf of children—to step back and examine their own behavior and long-held practices. Daniela Papi, co-founder of PEPY, a Cambodia-based education and youth leadership nonprofit, explained, "If your goal is fundraising, you actually have an incentive to pull out the most gory story. And so we get completely false realities of the world."[43] It's for this reason that, in the wake of the exposure of Mam's lies, nonprofits are making a concerted effort to stop using abused children as spokespeople, and fundraising tools, for their organizations.

In a previous era, the good that Somaly Mam did for girls and young women in Cambodia by providing a safe place to live and access to education and job training would have outweighed and outlived all her falsehoods. Perhaps the saddest truth about the Somaly Mam exposé is that she didn't need to make up stories to underscore the brutality and devastation of the sex-trafficking epidemic, not only in Cambodia, but around the world. The International Labour Organization estimates that 5.5 million children around the world are victims of forced labor, often trafficked for sexual exploitation, a trade that represents a $32 billion dollar business.[44] Author Audre Lorde once wrote, "The master's tools will never dismantle the master's house. They may allow us to temporarily beat him at his own game, but they will never enable us to bring about genuine change."[45] This seems especially true for Somaly Mam, whose decades of documented activism against a system built on deception and illegal activity was stopped in its own do-good tracks by her own web of lies.

Mam used her connectional intelligence to build an organization that spotlighted horrific crimes and saved thousands of girls. But her story shows that there is a dark side to the power that you experience when your connectional intelligence combusts across the globe into big results. The pull, desire and demands of "going big" and "sustaining big" can cause some people to waver, to take a step over the line of truth. At first, it's just a little waver, a moment of convenience. But like a rip tide lurking in the sea, once you put your toe in, the deception pulls you in deeper, until it's eventually almost impossible to break free.

It will be an interesting test of our connectional intelligence—and theirs—to see if and how we are willing to move past the wrongdoings of Armstrong and Mam and find a way they can again use their gifts for good.

6

CONNECT AND
MAKE CHANGE

HUNTER HOFFMAN BEGAN HIS RESEARCH CAREER AT Princeton as a cognitive psychologist whose work measured the mind's ability to distinguish between real and false memories. At the University of Washington Human Interface Technology Lab in Seattle, he and two clinical psychology therapists recruited patients who feared spiders, then had them play a game he designed called *Spider World*. Before playing the game, some patients were so terrified of spiders they sealed their windows. But when they wore virtual-reality goggles, guided and reassured by their therapist, patients found they could move "closer" to spiders—virtual spiders, at least. In the virtual world, fears, even deeply held ones, dissipated.[1]

Early in his career, Hunter was chatting with a friend who was doing research on pain management for burn victims. "They were using hypnosis," Hunter recalled in an interview with the authors, "but they didn't *really* know how it worked on the brain. I remember my friend saying, 'We don't really know, but it seems to have something to do with distraction.'"[2] The minute his friend used the word "distraction," Hunter said, he jumped out of his chair and said, "*Whoa,* do I have a distraction for you."[3]

The two friends decided to try virtual-reality games as a way of distracting burn patients during often painful treatments. Hunter's grad student friend introduced him to a professor who was working at Harborview Burn Center. At the time, Hunter was in the engineering department at the University of Washington, which had a giant virtual-reality research center. Hunter still gets breathless when he talks about the excitement of hauling his equipment over to Harborview. Initially, they decided that it made sense to test the treatment on children, who understood more instinctively how virtual-reality games worked and were perhaps more willing to suspend disbelief and allow themselves to make believe they were inside the computer-generated virtual world.

Hunter and the professor at Harborview ran a controlled experiment. While a teenage patient with severe burns was having five staples removed from a skin graft, he had the boy play Nintendo *Mario Kart.* Then Hunter had him play *Spider World* during the removal of the other six staples. Which was more effective at reducing the teen's suffering? *Spider World.* The reason, Hunter believed, was that his virtual-reality game had more "presence"—the player really felt he was immersed in the world of the game. This allowed the boy's entire nervous system to be *deeply* distracted—to the point of barely noticing the very real and intense physical pain of the surgery. Hunter shakes his head with wonder at how a series of seemingly random conversations created connections that defined his life's work. "From the very first patient that we tried it on, it worked surprisingly well."[4] Still, building the pet project into a financially and academically sustainable research arena was a slow process. Hunter and the team at the Harborview Burn Center worked for free, for several years, to assemble the pilot data that would help them go big with their project (now funded by the National Institutes of Health).[5]

In the right environment, connectional intelligence can transform and diminish pain itself.

Burn patients were an intriguing subject because their care can, and often does, compound the trauma of the incident or series of incidents that caused their wounds. "Their pain levels are very high," Hunter explained. "They've had a painful experience, so they expect treatment to be painful as well. They're looking at the burn wound as the nurse cleans it. They are preoccupied with pain during wound care. The video game must be involving enough to isolate them from the real world so they can't see the wound care anymore. Beyond that, the game must be compelling enough to captivate their entire nervous system and transport them into another reality."[6]

In particular, the treatment of children with severe burns is full of suffering. Every day, for months on end, they have to endure painful cleansing of their wounds. The anticipation of the pain becomes a form of psychological suffering as well as physical. Pain medication is only partially effective, and doctors can only prescribe it in small doses, as pain medicine can be dangerous to children. Hunter's team found that *Spider World* was an especially powerful tool for helping kids who couldn't safely take the level of medicine that would stop their pain.

Despite the heavy-duty unpaid hours of research he put into those early years, Hunter recalled, the work was—from the beginning—intensely satisfying. "We got some *gorgeous* data showing huge reduction in pain," he said, describing the cortex scans that helped his team document that the games were working. "The brain really lit up like a

Christmas tree during pain, but during pain coupled with virtual reality, the pain-related brain activity dropped. Virtual reality, combined with the medicine, were [sic] better than either alone."[7]

He also learned that connection to another human being during the game lowered the experience of pain even more. "Having another person in the virtual world with you makes it a more compelling illusion," Hunter said. "And the kids like it best when their mother or someone close to them can join them in that virtual world."[8] How many times has a parent of a severely injured child thought, "If only I could experience that pain for you?" Hunter's game doesn't allow parents and caregivers to take away their children's pain, but by letting the child and caregiver connect through virtual reality during the treatment, a powerful bond is built and nurtured. Connectional intelligence not only helped Hunter innovate a game-changing solution to a problem that has haunted scientists and doctors for decades, he discovered it is also an integral part of the effective solution.

Connectional intelligence spans the power of both the brain and the heart—bringing us closer to each other, building our muscles of empathy and compassion and making us feel less alone. And in the right environment, connectional intelligence can transform and diminish pain itself.

"How alone are we in our suffering?" is one of the cornerstone questions of the human experience. Seeing a child isolated in pain, as Hunter discovered, is one of the most devastating things we can experience.

One day after school, after a day of bullying that had become a constant that neither his teachers nor the school's administrators could stop, Noah Brocklebank, a seventh grader from Columbia, Maryland, logged onto his Instagram to announce his intention to kill himself. After years of unrelenting bullying, after not being able to talk back to or fight back against kids who insisted he was "fat," "ugly," "annoying" and a "loser," Noah had begun self-mutilating. He posted photos of his bloodied arms on Instagram, then this note: "Day of scheduled suicide, February 8th, 2013, my birthday."[9]

One of the questions connectional intelligence seeks to solve is: How alone are we in our suffering?

For months, Noah's mother Karen Brocklebank had asked school parents and police officials for help, but no one seemed able to intervene. When she saw the note and heard about Noah's Instagram post from friends, she had twelve-year-old Noah admitted to the hospital. But she didn't stop there. Determined to do everything she could to help her son, she realized she would need the help of everyone she could find. She created a website, lettersfornoah.com, and urged Facebook friends to help.[10]

"I thought of it last night in the ER when I couldn't sleep," she posted. "Noah needs to know that he matters and that it does get better. So many people have been asking me how they can help. Well, this is how. Today I opened a P.O. Box. I am asking you and your kids to send Noah letters with a message of hope, telling him not to give up. Help him see that he matters."[11]

Karen Brocklebank expected a few letters; what she got was hundreds and hundreds of letters and cards from everyone from depression survivors and retirees, to whole first grade classrooms. Two weeks later, on his birthday, Noah had received 2,000 letters. On Facebook, he had 15,000 new "friends." This outpouring touched Noah: he started to understand that he was not as alone as he once thought.[12]

In traditional media, the story would end there—with a happy ending, with perhaps a follow-up story on Noah's next birthday. But in reality, it was still very tough sledding. Noah got out of the hospital and had to go back to school.

The bullying continued. Two months after Noah's birthday, he was back in the hospital. Karen never wavered in her crusade. The letters poured in, and they mattered. One of the most meaningful letters Noah received was from his fourth-grade teacher, who wrote: "I remember you fondly—humorous, smart, creative, fun to be around. . . . Life gets real good! But you have to get past the hard parts to reach the best parts."[13] Noah slowly began to feel he mattered—and that there was a vast world outside of his misery at school. He made it to the end of the school year.

Because Karen Brocklebank now considered herself in a relationship with thousands of virtual supporters, she posted an update on Facebook:

"Please, let Noah's story be a lesson to us all that it is always ok to ask for HELP when we need it. He was not 'attention seeking,' he was drowning and he needed a lifeline. I wasn't doing enough up until that point. The school wasn't helping. The parents were making it worse. Law enforcement said it was out of their hands. I had to fight hard to set him back on the path of happiness and security. We are here to tell you, NEVER GIVE UP. I never will, not until our kids feel safe and stop dying because of bullying. Not until the adults get it."[14]

In the fall, Noah switched schools.

"This is going to be my best year ever!" he announced.[15]

On February 8, 2014, his mother posted again.

"Can you believe it? Today is Noah's 14th birthday!!!! I am happy to say it is a much less eventful celebration than we had a year ago. Thank you all from the bottom of my heart for being here for us and continuing to remember and support Noah."[16]

What's the takeaway? First, many of us will struggle at some time in our life with feeling profoundly alone. Once you see the thousands of letters for Noah, you begin to understand that today's connectional intelligence means that there are new and powerful ways in which you (or those who care about you) can create a large and powerful web of support in your hardest times. And we've come to understand that listening—even listening closely and attentively—is not all that's required of us. Listening is also a call to act, even when the action that's indicated is uncomfortable, and we're so busy we "don't really have time." Today, we can act at scale in broader and deeper ways, even through small gestures. When many of us act, our small tokens are amplified into much greater impact. We can find the time to do small things when we know and feel that the impact of the whole will indeed be much bigger than the sum of the parts. We are connected at many levels—from friends, to families, to colleagues, to communities and companies; and in the end, we're responsible for ourselves and for each other.

When Allana Maiden was six years old, her mother was diagnosed with breast cancer. "Mom never complained," Allana recalled in an interview. "She didn't get depressed, she underwent a mastectomy, lost her hair."[17] The fight paid off. Allana's mother, Debbie Barrett, is a success story: today she's cancer-free. She went back to her life with passion and gratitude. But there were still obstacles. She didn't live in a city, and there was no local shop that sold post-mastectomy bras. She needed to be fitted, so she couldn't shop online. The closest solution required her to drive two hours away to get to a specialty store.

When Allana was twenty-eight, she decided there was something she could do for her mother. And she knew just who could help her: Victoria's Secret. The lingerie retailer had an outlet in every mall in America. A little research led her to a blog post that discussed a letter to Victoria's Secret that had suggested the lingerie company start making mastectomy bras. But it didn't seem as if the request had made much impact. Maybe, Allana thought, the idea needed more push.

She had no experience with online petitions, but she'd seen a story about a girl's wish for a gender-neutral easy bake oven for her brother. Change.org got involved; change happened, and the girl got her wish. So Allana decided to post a petition on Change.org. Change.org responded a day later; together they came up with the concept for a "survivor bra."

The first week the petition was online, Allana e-mailed it to every-one she knew: her mother, her friends, her co-workers. She posted it on Facebook—several times a day—and "tagged" anyone she thought might be interested. She posted it on the Susan G. Komen breast cancer awareness site, the American Cancer Society website and sites of other organizations. She posted it on Pinterest: "I wasn't sure how that would work, but a lot of things get passed around on Pinterest."[18]

The work she did shows how much reach one motivated individual can have when she seeks to connect with depth and purpose. "I worked with Change.org to ensure that every time someone signed the petition, an e-mail went to Victoria's Secret. We drafted a press release. Within a few weeks I was spending a whole day talking to reporters and we had over 100,000 signatures. I also reached out to Victoria's Secret and they put me in touch with the VP of communications. She asked the reporter for my contact info and we spoke on why I was running the campaign."[19]

When 120,000 people had signed the petition, things changed, and the vice president of communications at Victoria's Secret flew in from Columbus to meet with Allana.

"I wasn't really sure what to expect," Allana said, "but it's good to know that I've caught the ear of somebody who's higher up in the company and it really seems like they're interested in finding out more about this."[20]

In that first meeting, Allana learned that Victoria's Secret had re-searched possible designs for a mastectomy bra, but no mastectomy bra products were seriously being developed.

Victoria's Secret offered to fly Allana and Debbie to the company's headquarters in Columbus, Ohio to meet with more company officials. They went. They told their story. And they learned more about the work Victoria's Secret was doing, and the challenges they faced. In some ways it was disappointing. Victoria's Secret didn't create a survivor's bra, and maybe they never will.

That doesn't mean Allana's campaign was for naught. It was a powerful reminder that there is more we can do for the survivors of breast cancer. It made the conversation newly fresh and relevant for many survivors and their families. It encouraged families to keep asking how they can make sure their loved ones have the tools to not just survive, but thrive. And perhaps the most important outcome of Allana's campaign is that by taking the project of a survivor bra to the world at large, Allana created connections with over 100,000 people who shared her concern and caring. This created a ripple effect of connection that added new dimensions to the lives of both Allana and her mother. In the end, it strengthened their already deep bond.

Sugata Mitra began his scientific career studying molecular orbital computation. He moved on to research energy storage systems, then the flow of electricity in the human body, then the ways simulated neural networks can help us track Alzheimer's disease. Then he moved on to education and a study of hyperlinks, learning styles and learning devices; soon he was recognized as an educational innovator. Sugata saw the possibility for learning in every person—no matter their background or social status. And he was well-acquainted with and passionate about the formidable challenge of creating quality education for all in India.[21]

India's population is growing, and growing fast. By 2028, India is likely to be home to about as many people as China: 1.45 billion.[22] By 2038, India may be the most populous country on the planet. This creates a deep need for investment in its educational system. But that's simply not enough. Incremental change just isn't going to work.

"If a teacher can be replaced with a machine, he should be."[23] That's what Arthur C. Clarke, the novelist who wrote the book that became the movie *2001: Space Odyssey,* told Mitra in a conversation. For Clarke, the most important factor in education wasn't the presence of a teacher, but the interest and curiosity of a student.

Sugata was captivated by this idea and wanted to test it in a learning environment that most people thought to be hopeless. In 1999, he inserted a computer in the wall of a slum in Delhi, linked it to the Internet and left. And he repeated the experiment—which he called the "Hole in the Wall"—in a few villages. The result was the same. Without prompting and with no prior Internet experience, children began using the computers. They recorded music and played it back. They organized their own learning.

"The Victorians were great engineers," Sugata said. "They engineered a [schooling] system that was so robust that it's still with us today, continuously producing identical people for a world that no longer exists. So it's become quite fashionable to say that the education system's broken— it's not broken, it's wonderfully constructed. It's just that it's outdated. Now we know better: education in today's connected world can be a self-organizing system, where learning is an emergent phenomenon."[24]

There are now more than twenty-three Hole in the Wall kiosks in rural India. Sugata has won awards. And his kiosks are going global, with the same outcomes: higher test scores for students who interact with them. In Mexico, for example, a twelve-year-old girl from a slum won a national math contest after working with a Hole in the Wall– inspired math program conducted by an innovative instructor. And her entire class advanced from 0 to 63 percent in the excellent category in math.[25]

When you supersize the spark of shared interest with inclusive connection, imagine the possibilities this creates both for our aging populations and for our youth.

As word spread about what Sugata was doing, some grandmothers in England took notice and wanted to be part of it. Touched by their interest, Sugata created a way for them to get involved, and the "Granny Cloud"—a cadre of English and Australian grandmothers who Skype weekly with Indian children through the Hole in the Wall kiosks—was born. The grandmothers initially joined the project to play the traditional roles that grandmothers play everywhere—cheerleader, coach and storyteller. Sugata believes the addition of this human element, and exposure to a different way of looking at the world, can lead to a 25 percent increase in test scores. And most importantly, the kids loved it![26]

At first glance, it might appear that the grannies were the givers. But the truth is that there were huge and complementary benefits to both communities. The women in the "Granny Cloud" shared the joy of knowing wonderful children and seeing them grow and progress. The children and the elderly women got to know each other. The grannies found many shared interests and formed new friends at a stage in life when many faced loss and loneliness. And, it turned out, this kind of active involvement and connection has health benefits for elder populations.

In her groundbreaking research, epidemiologist and geriatrician Dr. Linda Fried, founder of Experience Corps and currently Dean of the Mailman School of Public Health, showed that cadres of elders who engage in cross-generational learning communities, similar to the "Granny Cloud," have decreased rates of physical disability and cognitive decline as they age.[27] When you supersize this by adding inclusive connection, virtual meetings with video and the self-organizing spark of shared interest and curiosity, imagine the possibilities created both for our aging populations and for our youth.

Martha Payne, a Scottish schoolgirl, was only nine years old when she launched her blog, NeverSeconds. Her goal was to document the sad state of cafeteria lunches at her primary school in western Scotland. Like Allana Maiden, Martha's goal was simple: to elevate the quality of life in her small part of the world, in a specific, but significant way.

Martha's first lunch post showed a photo of a discolored pizza slice that seemed to have spent much of its existence under a heat lamp, a once-frozen, warmed-over potato croquette and thirty kernels of canned corn that had lost their color, and, one assumes, their nutritional value. For this meal, Martha's parents were charged £2, or about $3.25.[28] Not exactly a bargain.

An incredulous Martha wrote, "I'm a growing kid, and I need to concentrate all afternoon. I can't do it on one croquette. Do any of you think you could?"[29]

Soon NeverSeconds was racing toward two million visits, and a reporter from the local paper and some government officials visited the school. Lunch that day was a very different meal from the ones that inspired Martha to start her blog. Martha chronicled what she had been served, describing the fresh vegetables and their bright pops of color the way an average kid might describe a plate full of candy. "For the first time ever I have seen at lunch cherry tomatoes, radishes, carrot and cucumber shreddings," she marveled. She also noted a marked improvement in the attitude of the school cafeteria workers who asked, also for the first time, if Martha had been given enough food and if she would like more. Excitedly, she wrote, "I hope it will be the same tomorrow."[30]

The ranks of Martha's fans grew to include celebrity chef Jamie Oliver, who had formed a foundation dedicated to what he called a "school food revolution." Nearly a decade before, Oliver had taken on the British school lunch system in an award-winning documentary series called "Jamie's School Dinners." ("School Dinners" is the British term for school lunches.) In the series, Oliver set up camp as resident cook in a school in Greenwich, England where he discovered, to his horror, that despite what parents were being charged, the school was spending a miserly 37 pence (61 cents) per student on the school lunches.[31] The series provoked outrage throughout Britain, and the prime minister, Tony Blair himself, promised to help. The result was massive: junk food (chips, soda, etc.) were banned in British public schools and the government established a £60 million initiative to improve school lunches. And yet, just an eight-hour drive north in Scotland, Martha Payne couldn't get a decent meal at lunch time.

Jamie Oliver tweeted about Martha and sent her a personal message of support, "Great work! Clever girl—Keep it up!"[32]

But it wasn't easy to keep up. The day after the media visited her school for the farmer's-market inspired lunch that included cherry tomatoes, radishes, carrots and cucumber, Martha was shocked to see that, with all the cameras gone, it was business as usual in her school cafeteria.

Lunch the next day consisted of a watered-down soup, a roll, four slices of cucumber and a few lettuce leaves, followed by a tiny pudding. Naturally, she blogged about it: "The new things from yesterday, the radishes, the mini tomatoes and the shreddings weren't to be seen today. Maybe it was just because my class was last in the queue and I was the last in the school to be served. I was looking forward to the radishes because I have not had one for a while."[33]

The local newspaper amplified her report, and wondered:

Could it be possible that an education authority charged with the precious and vital task of feeding our children gave them better grub only when someone was watching them? Surely not. That would be like the fat beadle in *Oliver Twist* giving the orphans in his care a fine roast chicken dinner during an Ofsted [the British equivalent of the Department of Child Welfare] inspection and putting them back on watery gruel the day after.[34]

The local council's executive director for education, Cleland Sneddon—a name right out of a nineteenth century novel—had Martha called out of class. She could not be prevented from blogging, but she could be forbidden to take pictures of her lunch. As Mr. Sneddon explained it to Martha's father, she had "misrepresented" the school dinner choices—Martha had simply not availed herself of fruit and vegetables. The council continued its offensive: "We haven't had a single complaint in two years, you can see the quality of our service. Some of her blogs we believe were highly critical and not representative."[35]

Martha's response was to publish photographs sent by kids around the world, showing their school lunches. As a newspaper report noted, the global revolution in school lunches was a long way away from taking root in Scotland. In the photos the other kids sent to Martha the reporter saw: "Mouthwatering pictures of falafel from Israel, pumpkin cheesecake from Canada, sausage and vegetable soup from Finland, sushi from Japan and even in America, where we are told junk food is making everyone obese, there were beef tacos, rice, noodle soup, sunflower seeds, hummus and an apple."[36]

Martha broadened her blog. She wrote to the company that supplied hot dogs to her school—and learned that those wieners had been processed and canned up to three years earlier. Naturally she published that response.

Martha's blog was now global. Martha's campaign followed suit. She used her platform to raise almost $100,000 to build a new kitchen in a poor Malawi village. In 2012, she traveled more than 5,000 miles to see the effect of her speaking up and speaking out. She wrote:

> When we arrived, nearly 2,000 children were lined up outside and they sang as I was introduced to the headmistress. I could feel the song in my chest because it was so loud. Dad, Mum and Grandpa had tears in their eyes and I had to squeeze Dad's hand.
>
> When the children went into class, I went to the new kitchen . . . There were six massive pots of porridge being cooked and the ladies were

singing as they stirred it. . . . Outside was a sign which I helped to paint. I wrote "NeverSeconds" in blue paint with help from my brother and sister. All together it says: "Mary's Meals Centre—Lirangwe. Kindly donated by Friends of NeverSeconds."[37]

Although she was very young, Martha displayed high levels of connectional intelligence. She created a blog, to not only improve the quality of her own lunch, but to raise the bar on school meals for all of the kids in her school. When celebrity came, she remained focused on her mission, to bring fresh and healthier meals to school cafeterias. She understood how to connect and engage multiple groups, to bring fresh perspectives from the outside and to continue a courageous conversation, despite great pressure to be silenced.

Martha understood that the question of school food had implications way beyond Scotland. When donations began pouring in to the blog, she redirected the funds to Malawi. She knew that a revolution in school lunches there was much more basic in scope, that it was an ongoing campaign to get kids into the classroom and a fight to make sure they receive enough food to make it through the day.

We've said before that courage builds on courage, but it is also true that connection builds on connection. When we look for it, there are literally hundreds of ways to plug in and partner with the hundreds of thousands of men, women and even children who share our common goals.

The daughter of an American father and a Columbian mother, Maria Theresa Kumar believed she was born to run Voto Latino, the nonprofit she helped to create. "I grew up in a bi-cultural household, so my whole life I have been translating," she says. "And with Voto Latino, it is about translating to mainstream America what it means to be Latino."[38] The organization's mission is to help young Latinos recognize the power of their vote and to help Washington power brokers understand what a force the growing Latino community is.

Voto Latino began as a series of Latino-geared television public service announcements (PSAs), created by actress Rosario Dawson, the organization's co-founder, during the 2004 election. When Dawson met
Maria, the latter knew right away that the PSAs could be more than just
engaging content. Maria believed that they could be a launching pad for
an organization that would be the voice of the growing, largely bipar-
tisan, Latino community. "We always meant to target the children of
immigrants," Maria explained. "Long before we turn 18, we are playing
leadership roles in our family. Often we're the only ones who speak English in the home. We literally translate the world for our parents. Once
we get these young people involved, their potential for influence is huge.
The big question is, how do we as Americans and Latinos participate in
the political process?"[39]

Maria was completing her master's in public policy at Harvard's
Kennedy School of Government at the time. Although she had many
job offers, she felt deeply that Voto Latino was her calling. So she moved
back home to California and began the organization in her childhood
bedroom. "My mom understood my desire to make a difference," she
said.[40]

The stats are powerful. There are more than 15 million American
Latino youth in the United States, but historically only a small percentage of the community votes in local and national elections. Every
month, 66,000 Latinos turn 18. Many share the values and concerns
of both the Republican and Democratic parties. Latinos already make
up 10 percent or more of the voting electorate in eleven states including
Arizona, California, New York, Florida and Texas.

Using thoughtful, bilingual social media campaigns, Voto Latino
helped register hundreds of thousands of Latinos across the country,
sometimes as many as 3,000 in a single day. The group created a bilingual app for the 2010 Census and engaged thousands of Latinos in its
Affordable Health Care Google Hangouts.

*Young Latinos literally translate the world for
their parents. Their potential for influence is huge.
The big question is: How do we participate?*

Maria is aware that while voting has been a big win for Voto Latino, there are other issues of vast importance to her community that need to be addressed—immigration reform and unemployment are chief among them. But she believes the organization is just getting started. "My grandmother from Colombia always said, *'No* is for everybody else,'" she explained. "Meaning, if you work hard, you may hear *no* a hundred times. But eventually you'll find an ally who says *yes.*"[41] Imagine what might happen when Voto Latino and Maria Kumar combine those yeses across their networks of connectional intelligence—in school, work and play. It will be the kind of force-multiplier that Maria Kumar will need as she reaches for her big dream of creating translation from one culture to the next, weaving an interconnected fabric of diverse civic society for the generations to come.

7

PROBLEM SOLVING AND THE POWER OF PLAY

CONNECTIONAL INTELLIGENCE ISN'T ONLY ABOUT SHARING ideas, data and problems with lots of other people. It's also about the ability to *design problems* in such a way that many people will want to pitch in to solve them.

The British Parliament expense scandal, which began in 2009, transformed thousands of citizens from outraged newspaper readers into deputized journalists and brought down a system that had gone unchecked for generations.

For decades, members of Parliament (MPs) could claim expenses "wholly, exclusively and necessarily incurred for the performance of a Member's parliamentary duties."[1] That wonderfully vague language—coupled with almost nonexistent oversight—was a delight to MPs who lived far from London and, as a result, needed an in-town residence while parliament was in session. Inevitably, MPs took advantage: they used taxpayer money to rent apartments in upscale neighborhoods, buy property, furnish and renovate existing property and, in many cases, this money covered everything from gardening costs to swimming pool repairs.

Connectional intelligence includes the ability to design problems in a way that many people will want to pitch in and solve them.

In 2005, that began to change: Britain's Freedom of Information Act allowed the public to seek disclosure of expense information from the government. Some MPs fought the request but ultimately the court ordered them to release the expense information with "sensitive data" removed.[2] In 2009, two months before the official release of the report of MP expenses from 2004 to 2008, the full and *uncensored* report was leaked to *The Daily Telegraph*, which promptly published it in a searchable database detailing all of the MPs' expenses.[3]

For members of Parliament, the timing couldn't have been worse. The government was unpopular. There was a severe economic crisis. The public was eager for blood. When *Question Time,* a public affairs TV show, devoted an episode to the scandal, it scored the highest rating in its thirty-year history.[4]

The Telegraph's archenemy, *The Guardian,* also joined the fray, posting a spreadsheet online that listed all 646 MPs and their expenses, and inviting their readers to dig in: "Now that the receipts are—finally—published today, have you lost track of who claimed what, who paid it back, who got sacked and who resigned? Well, this is the place to start."[5]

The list was long and the offenses were egregious:

1. John Prescott, former deputy prime minister, claimed more than £635 ($1,040) for mock Tudor beams and two new toilet seats.[6]

2. David Milliband, foreign secretary, claimed just under £30,000 ($49,100) in gardening expenses, repairs, decorations and furniture for his family home.[7]

3. Phil Woolas, the immigration minister, was alleged to have claimed expenses for women's clothing, comic books and diapers.[8]

4. Michael Ancram, the independently wealthy Conservative Parliament member who held the title of the Marquess of Lothian, had claimed £98 ($160) for a repair to his swimming pool heater.[9]

5. Bill Cash, whose name was an unfortunate target for headlines, had paid more than £15,000 ($25,550) in "rent" to his daughter for her Notting Hill apartment, despite the fact that he owned an apartment closer to the Parliament offices. When confronted with the expense, Cash bristled that the money he had paid his daughter "was only for a year."[10]

The British people were outraged. In a country where the average family lives on an annual income of £26,500 ($43,370), the tens of thousands of taxpayer monies being used to supplement what were already lavish lifestyles was insulting.[11] In just eleven days, *The Telegraph*'s circulation soared by 600,000, and England found itself in the throes of its biggest political scandal in decades—so severe the news that then Prime Minister Gordon Brown had paid his brother for a shared cleaner and expensed a plumbing bill twice almost stopped the government. "It was awful," a Labor adviser recalled. "We lost 48 hours as he pored over his own case when we should have realized we were being hit by a tsunami."[12]

The Telegraph and its team of reporters had been working on the expenses scandal story for months. The public outcry was so great that the government released over a million documents and scanned receipts in an attempt to prove transparency and a lack of wrong-doing. But *The Guardian* also acted quickly, putting out a call for readers to join the newspaper's staff in sifting and analyzing the documents that had been released. "We hope that many hands can make light work of the thousands of documents released by Parliament in relation to MPs' expenses," read a statement on the *Guardian*'s website. "We, and others—perhaps you?—are using these tools to review each document, decide whether it contains interesting information, and extract the key facts."[13]

The response was immediate, the volume unprecedented. More than 20,000 readers reviewed 170,000 documents in four days.[14] Although the public's fury over the expenses scandal brought many to the *Guardian* website, the newspaper's web team knew that they needed to do more to keep the layman readers engaged. They created a four-panel interface that allowed the reader-reviewers to mark each document as "interesting," "not interesting," "interesting but known," or "investigate this!"

The web team added to the game-like aspect of reviewing the receipts by putting a progress bar on the home page of the site, uniting all of the reader-reviewers in the goal of hitting the big "score." Then *Guardian* staff parsed the data of the reader-reviewers so they could list "the top scorers" among the readers. This added to the rush to review data and to the motivation of the reader-reviewer "team," a disparate group of 20,000 individuals, each reader working solo from a home computer. As Simon Willison, the head developer at *The Guardian,* later told reporters, "Any time that you're trying to get people to give you stuff, to do stuff for you, the most important thing is that people know that what they're doing is having an effect. It's kind of a fundamental tenet of social software. . . . If you're not giving people the 'I rock' vibe, you're not getting people to stick around."[15]

The Guardian learned that adding a photo of the Parliament member whose receipts were being correlated helped drive up the engagement and efficiency of the readers reviewing the receipts. Simon later said, "You've got this big smiling face looking at you while you're digging through their expenses."[16] Finally, the UK paper reached out to Amazon, which rented them server space at a nominal fee to handle the overflow of data. In the end, apart from the staff already employed by the paper, the cost of this entire enterprise was only about £50 ($81) of incremental, unbudgeted expenses.[17]

Because of the *Guardian* team's ability to design the action, average citizens were able to participate directly and change the nature of the public sphere. The *Guardian* team coordinated and enabled a staggering expansion in the volume and range of opinions being expressed and work being contributed.

At the British Press Awards, *The Daily Telegraph* was named the "National Newspaper of the Year" for breaking news. But in the journalistic community it was largely believed that *The Guardian,* and its fast-thinking web team, got the bigger win.

Digital games have emerged as a powerful platform for connectional intelligence because the ability to process data quickly, make connections and solve problems are all hardwired into the DNA of the gaming culture. Games and tasks like the *Guardian* data-sift engage masses of people to unique tasks by testing their curiosity, while addressing real-world challenges.

In 2011, gamers playing *Foldit,* a program in which players compete and collaborate to manipulate protein shapes, solved a problem in three weeks that scientists had been working on for ten years. And not a small one, either: they solved a riddle about the shape of a protein related to AIDS in rhesus monkeys.

It's quite difficult to figure out the shape proteins will take. This is a fundamental problem of great importance to science, since proteins are one of the building blocks of life. Understanding protein shapes can lead to everything from new vaccines to better plastics. But identifying the protein shapes has always been a challenge.

When scientists try to understand a protein they look at its shape, which it takes through a process called folding. Unfortunately, proteins are so small it's impossible to determine their shape with a microscope. Instead, hundreds of millions of dollars are spent on special equipment and procedures to determine the shapes. Work typically involves taking potential protein shapes, making random changes and then comparing the old shapes to the new to see which is most likely to be the real shape of the protein. The number of potential real shapes taken by even the tiniest proteins is greater than the known stars in the universe. Discovering the true shape of a protein takes time, requires specialized training and doesn't always work.

Most of this work is done by scientists running complex programs on massive computers in research facilities. Applying techniques of parallel processing has allowed some of the work to be outsourced to amateurs who agree to run computations on their desktops in their downtime. But no matter how it's done, these computations still take an inordinate amount of time.

Foldit's creators, David Baker, David Salesin, Zoran Popovic, Seth Cooper and Adrian Treuille, knew that the power of play unlocks the human imagination in all sorts of unexpected ways. In a TED talk the summer after announcing *Foldit*'s breakthrough, co-founder Seth Cooper told the audience that "play is a space where people are free to experiment, to dream, and to be daring without the fear of failing. People are more willing to try new and crazy ideas when they're not concerned about the outcome."[18] And humans are, for now, still inherently better at certain types of creative problem-solving than computers.

Seth and his partners started with the principle that a really good way to solve challenging problems is to take the best of what humans and computers are capable of, and combine this to make something better. If the key advantage of humans over computers is creativity, then number-crunching is the computers' edge. But creativity, especially spatial reasoning, is a key to *Foldit*. Proteins are like 3-D jigsaw puzzles: all the pieces need to fit together in just the right way to work. Humans can see how proteins fit together (when greatly magnified) in a way computers just can't. It's the same ability you use when you look at a puzzle and see that the missing piece is the same shape as the one in your hand.

With over 200,000 players of the *Foldit* game, the founders set up a wiki and several *Foldit* chatrooms to engage gamers to discuss their favorite strategies and to share tips for the benefit of the group. Through the chatrooms, some gamers formed teams with names like *Void Crushers* and *Contenders* to help each other achieve high scores. The *Contenders* group described how this collaboration worked on the *FoldIt* website: "We play our soloist games our own way; but if someone finds sudden success, it's posted for the benefit of the group, detailing what was done to get there."[19]

In the case of the protein related to the AIDS virus, the gamers—few of whom had the biochemistry background that lab work would have required—test-folded the protein, grading and aiding one another along the way. For researchers, it was like fast-forwarding through a long and tedious movie to their favorite part. There was still work to do, but the complicated tests and calculations had been taken care of, thanks to the power of play. And AIDS isn't the only virus *Foldit* players can endeavor to illuminate. In 2014, as news of the Ebola crisis began making headlines, *Foldit* quickly added an Ebola game, allowing players to join the battle against this deadly virus.

Other games followed *Foldit*'s lead, including the desktop games *Nanocrafter*, a scientific discovery game about synthetic biology, and *EteRNA*, a browser-based game that engages users to solve problems related to the RNA gene molecules. Games like these even made their way to the mainstream. MIT's iPad app, *EyeWire*, a brain-mapping game, engaged players to map over one hundred real neurons. *Foldit* also evolved. Like any other digital game, its developers continually refined the metrics of play to increase time on the site, solve harder problems and give players a chance to refine their skills. If you play it now it's different than it was at launch.

Here we see connectional intelligence going beyond basic crowdsourcing. The creators of *Foldit* weren't just asking crowds to find a breakthrough solution. They designed good problem-solving through an effective gaming approach. This enabled large numbers to play, win, learn, share and create great science and at the same time, build and sustain a growing community that continued to solve new science challenges.

In 2008, a grassroots effort in Estonia called Let's Do It mobilized thousands of Estonians to do a massive cleanup of a widespread problem of trash that had been illegally dumped. The movement was the brainchild of Rainer Nõlvak, an Internet entrepreneur; twenty-six-year-old Tiina Urm; and Ahti Heinla, one of the founders of Skype. The team organized a crew of 720 volunteers who used their mobile phones to take photos and strategize the sites where the cleanup was most needed.[20]

In the end, more than 50,000 Estonians were able to accomplish a project that the Estonian government had estimated would take three years and cost 22.5 million euros. Let's Do It Estonia accomplished the task for just a fraction of the cost (just 500,000 euros) and even more incredibly, took less than half a day—just five hours.[21]

By capturing the cognitive surplus of individuals, the founders of Let's Do It have shown the world that connecting hearts, minds and data allows people to solve problems thought to be hopeless and intractable.

The idea spread from Estonia to all of Europe and beyond. There are now cleanup days in 110 countries, involving 10 million volunteers. In 2009, Latvians and Lithuanians cleaned up their countries with more than 250,000 people participating; they did it again in each of the next three years, engaging more people each year. On March 20, 2010, Portugal cleaned itself up, with the help of 200,000 people. Slovenia followed shortly, breaking all records with 270,000 people (13 percent of the country's population) taking part in the action.[22]

The Let's Do It campaign has now built the "World's Ugliest Map Ever," a map of the world's waste. Across the globe, users of the organization's free app for iPhones and Androids add to this map by sending pictures and location information about sites plagued by unwanted garbage. The result, an "open virtual world waste map," details the ugly truth on the Let's Do It website.[23] The Let's Do It team is currently working on a social network for mappers on which mappers can find each other, see what their friends have mapped and update each other's data. (At the time this book was published, the network was still under construction.)[24] By capturing the cognitive surplus of individuals, the founders of Estonia's Let's Do It have shown the world that connecting hearts, minds and data allows people to solve problems thought to be hopeless and intractable.

On the face of it, the plumbing business doesn't look like an industry ripe for innovation. But Anthony Gemma knew that some of the oldest industries are the ones that most need to evolve.

Anthony was only ten years old when he started working as a plumber's helper in his family's plumbing business. The youngest of nine children, he grew up in Providence, Rhode Island. His parents encouraged their children to pursue higher education but still required them to learn the nuts and bolts skills that had helped their working class family survive and thrive. Anthony went to college, then to law school and then returned to the family business, Gem Plumbing, as executive vice-president and CEO. Working with his brothers, Anthony was determined to transform the plumbing business into a model of corporate innovation. Their approach was to always look at their business from the perspective of connection—starting with customers. If they could connect with people, what would they learn? If they could see more, what would they want to know to connect the dots and create better service? What could they connect to dramatically improve both their customer's experience and their processes?

Anthony and his brothers began by collecting data on everything, from the location, cost and inventory of each part to how long a customer was put on hold before being connected to a live dispatcher. Then they looked at traffic patterns. Since plumbers only get paid for the hours they are on the job, too much time on the truck is money wasted; and customers hate it when plumbers are late.

They set up twelve-foot monitoring screens with real-time traffic reports and satellite feeds from every truck in the Gem fleet. This gave the brothers the data needed to eliminate lateness due to traffic.

In short order, their traffic data became so good they created a sideline source of income by supplying traffic stats to the Department of Transportation and local radio stations. They measured everything they could about the customer experience and continually used this data to make improvements wherever they could. Then they looked at media, tailoring their ad buys to availability spikes in their service fleets.[25]

When Anthony first joined the company after law school, Gem employed 80 people and had about $14 million dollars in annual sales. A decade later, Gem had grown to more than 300 employees with over $33 million in sales.[26] But what really caught on was the Gem business model. So many small businesses wanted to come and tour Gem Plumbing that the brothers set up the Gem Institute for Performance Excellence to share what the brothers had learned about using connection to drive innovation, efficiency, customer service and employee development. Anthony Gemma demonstrates that connectionally intelligent innovators aren't all tech whizzes or scientists; they pop up everywhere.

The everyday practicality of using games, technology and the power of crowd-sourcing to solve big problems is as applicable to traffic as it is to plumbing. There are cities where traffic is terrible, and then there is Cairo:

- Cairo has few parking lots, so drivers park in the streets, clogging traffic.
- Cairo has few stoplights.
- Cairo's drivers can get their licenses without a road test.
- Cairo's wider streets are three lanes, but drivers create five. The sides of their cars practically scrape.
- Cairo traffic is so snarled that ambulances are equipped with loudspeakers.
- Street vendors—there are thousands—have no place to go, so they set up their carts in the streets.[27]

The cost of Cairo's traffic snarl is high: as much as $8 billion a year—3 percent of the city's gross domestic product—in lost productivity, delays and excess fuel consumption.[28] The accident rate in Egypt is thirty-four times higher than that in Europe and three times as high as some other countries in the region, leading to major disorder on the roads.[29] You might think that Cairo, with over 18 million people and around 2.4 million cars, would make unclogging the city's traffic a priority. And it does, in its own way. Which is to say, not quickly.[30]

Into the gap stepped Gamal Sadek and four of his cousins. In 2010, these Cairo residents launched Bey2ollak, an app named for an Egyptian expression used when telling someone about something you've heard. The insight behind starting Bey2ollak: people reported traffic information informally using #CairoTraffic on Twitter. And a couple of radio traffic bulletins were broadcast daily. But there was a big gap between the misinformation on the public radio traffic updates and the real-time Twitter feeds from people actually on the road.

Gamal was inspired to create an application to organize the existing information and help local commuters navigate their daily road journeys and improve traffic. Bey2ollak's mission was described as: "a Cross Platform Mobile application for people to exchange info about traffic that uses the power of crowd-sourcing, social interaction, localization and above all simplicity with the vision of providing our users with the ideal road companion app on their everyday journey!"[31]

Translation: Bey2ollak uses a mobile application to get you where you want to go faster and with less aggravation by alerting you to traffic issues and allowing you to share real-time updates and to interact with fellow Egyptian commuters.

People in Cairo embraced Bey2ollak right away—on October 10, the launch day, the app went viral with around 6,000 users signing up. On the second day, Vodafone Egypt reached out to help, spreading the word to its customers.[32]

Today, Bey2ollak has over one million registered users and is the eighth most popular and important brand in Egypt with over 250,000 fans on Facebook and 110,000 Twitter followers.[33]

But alerting people to traffic issues is just Bey2ollak's role on an ordinary day.

During the early stages of the Tahrir Square protests in 2011, after Facebook and Twitter were banned in Egypt, Bey2ollak users used the application to self-organize communities to certain locations. As Gamal described, "We started reporting blocked roads and adding more features like khatar (danger) to warn about unsafe roads and Elhaany (help me) that tracked the numbers of the emergency services."[34]

In 2013, there was a gas crisis: lines at gas stations were so long that drivers sometimes waited all night for fuel. Bey2ollak users collaborated through the app and helped each other find out which gas stations were closed and which had ample supplies. Bey2ollak has also been used to allow citizens to identify "hot spots" of major traffic, highlight the need to fix the roads over time and make suggestions for alternative routes.

The application is no longer just about traffic, it is used to alert citizens about anything that happens on the roads, from dance events to festivals to Ramadan gatherings—really, anything that happens on the streets of Cairo that might cause traffic.

The company is built on a "trust-based network" with its users, meaning that it collects contributions from users about the traffic where they are and evaluates the reports according to information about the user and how many times they have shared information. "We rank users from 'unsure' to 'top reporters' when deciding what to tell our other users about the traffic," Gamal said. "If wrong information is shared, we can take various measures from warning to blocking a user from reporting."[35]

In the mobile app industry, Bey2ollak is considered a huge success.

"We want to help each other, and improve the entrepreneurial society in Egypt, because this is the future,"[36] Gamal said. Gamal became a leading force to many Egyptians, because he used inclusive connection and connectional intelligence. He became a practical visionary, creating a way for people stuck in Cairo traffic to pinpoint problems, make them visible to everyone and improve and track solutions.

"We have to take part in this ourselves if we want to make Egypt a better place," Gamal said.[37]

That message resonates with people around the world.

In India, where 600 million people live in rural communities, agricultural instruction is essential. A spate of bad crops or a widespread infestation can have devastating effects. For decades, the Ministry of

Agriculture dutifully made and broadcast how-to videos, hoping to help farmers do their best work. But the videos had many problems, not the least of which was that India is a diverse country with vast cultural and ethnic differences. They simply did not translate across the different farming communities.

That is, until Rikin Gandhi, a twenty-nine-year-old researcher at Microsoft India, came up with the idea of Digital Green, which puts the farmer in the director's chair. By providing farmers with phones and hand-held cameras, Digital Green enables them to create low-cost, how-to videos on farming strategies and techniques. They address questions like, "How do you select a crop? How do you prepare your land and nursery beds? How do you transplant crops? How do you remove weeds to get a healthier crop?"[38] The resulting videos, which run eight-to-ten minutes, showcase and share the farmers' expertise and empower this new breed of farmer-filmmakers.

Once completed, Digital Green and partnering NGOs review each film for quality and accuracy. Then, using handheld projectors, they hold screenings in villages.

During these events, Rikin notes: "The first questions we get are 'what are the names of the farmers in the video?' and 'which village is he or she from?'—that's before we even talk about the agricultural practice, they want to know who these people are."[39] That inspired Rikin to create Farmerbook, a social networking platform for farmers.

"As these interactions are happening, they are recording who gives a thumbs up to a video, what questions if any they ask, which videos are being screened, and which practices are adopted on their farms," Rikin said. "We plot these farmers on a Google map, and you can jump into each individual village and see all these farmers we work with—which videos that this woman in this village has seen over the course of time."[40]

Farmerbook now boasts an impressive library of over 2,500 You-Tube videos in twenty different languages. On the site, viewers can sort the videos to find those that give specific information about their district, the type of farming they are doing and the crops they are growing. Rikin and his team have "created a leaderboard among the farmers so they can compare themselves among each other. It's based on the adoption rate—the number of practices adopted relative to each video they've seen."[41] Farmerbook also includes profiles of facilitators, enabling the NGOs who hire them to track effectiveness.

Digital Green has been far more successful than the existing government-sponsored program. In fact, when compared with this program, for every dollar spent, Digital Green has persuaded seven times as many farmers to adopt new practices. Digital Green has expanded its "YouTube meets American Idol" format to Ghana and Ethiopia. The data collected by the project and Farmerbook is saving money for NGOs, which can now track the effectiveness of the projects they manage and make appropriate, informed changes to those that aren't working. Participation is widespread and enthusiastic; more than 125,000 farmers from 1,500 villages are working with Digital Green today.[42]

Rikin Gandhi is a prime example of what connectionally intelligent millennials have to offer old-school fields like agriculture. He designed a system that combines a variety of connectional techniques from mid-tech (video, phones) to low-tech connection (physical gatherings led by facilitators) that is improving the farmers' adoption of new techniques sevenfold. He uses the video "inversion" concept, like that used in the Khan Academy (see chapter 3), to improve the effectiveness and enhance the adoption of lessons by tracking what questions farmers ask, which videos are being screened and which practices are adopted on the farms. He uses his connectional and emotional intelligence to navigate the cultural and ethnic differences of farmers and their mistrust of government workers. He activates the connectional intelligence of the members of the ecosystem through Farmerbook, which allows farmers to connect directly to one another based on their village and language. He also uses data collected from the project and Farmerbook to enable NGO members to make better project decisions. He's still so young. It will be fascinating to watch how Rikin Gandhi's work develops across a wide set of issues, including health and sanitation.[43]

As we study the evolution of connectional intelligence, we see that often a person begins with one purpose, which leads to other—unexpected—results.

For Luis von Ahn, making a difference is what matters most. He says that the focus of his research and work is in the Venn diagram of "systems that combine human brainpower and computers to solve large scale problems that neither can solve alone."[44] But it goes further than that. Luis is a pioneer in the field of crowd-sourcing. He has a mind that creatively frames solutions not on the brain power of a single person working with a computer, but on the exponential power of hundreds of thousands of people using computers to complete simple tasks we all do every day.

As a twenty-one-year-old graduate student at Carnegie Mellon University, he helped create CAPTCHA, an acronym that stands for Completely Automated Public Turing test to tell Computers and Humans Apart. A CAPTCHA is the distorted series of characters you are asked to type in on web forms or sites like Ticketmaster. As you type the CAPTCHA, you prove to the computer that you are a human and not a program designed to fill out the form over and over again. On a site like Ticketmaster, for example, the CAPTCHA prevents scalpers from programming computers to buy hundreds of tickets within minutes and scalping them for a much higher price.

CAPTCHA was a pretty cool project. But Luis was just getting started. He learned that 200 million CAPTCHAs are typed around the world every day and that it takes about ten seconds to type each one. And then, because he's a scientist, he did the math: 200 million CAPTCHAs at ten seconds each translated into 500,000 hours of wasted time.[45]

There are many problems, Luis reasoned, that are too big or arduous for an individual, team, or even a small community of a few hundred to be able to solve. What if he could break one of those problems into ten-second tasks that people all over the world could work on together? Luis came up with a powerful answer: digitizing books. It turns out that scanning books, the most common way to digitize a physical book, is remarkably inefficient. The scan is a picture of the words on the page, but computers don't have a quick, accurate way to recognize all of the words. The older the book, the more inaccurate the read. For books that are more than fifty years old, the inaccuracy rate can be as high as 30 percent or more. Luis's next venture, reCAPTCHA, takes the words from older books that the computer couldn't recognize and turns them into CAPTCHAs. Now when you see two words on a web security screen, one of the words is actually a CAPTCHA of a word that the digital library system found in a book, did not recognize and is presenting to you to help generate a correct answer. The other word is a standard CAPTCHA that verifies that you are indeed, a human. When lots of people type the same string of characters for the word the digital library didn't recognize, Luis's system accepts this string as a valid digitization of the word, and thus an old book comes closer to living accurately in digital form. ReCAPTCHA is now used on thousands of sites including Facebook and Twitter, which means roughly 100 million words are being identified each day and your ten-second contribution is going toward the digitization of two and a half million books a year.[46]

Luis von Ahn's next goal was to translate the vast body of knowledge on the web into as many languages as possible. There are translation tools, like Google Translate, but as Luis knows, the technology just isn't good enough, and won't be for at least another fifteen to twenty years. Even the best online translation tools make a lot of mistakes. During a TEDx talk at Carnegie Mellon, Luis gave an example of the pitfalls of translating tools, in a Japanese person's attempt to use an online tool to translate a question about Java script from Japanese into English:

> The Japanese person began her question and right away, it was clear that there were errors in the tool's translation: "At often, the goat time install a error is vomit."
>
> Then she posed another question: "How many times like the wind, a pole and the dragon?"
>
> Another question: "This insult to father's stones?"
>
> And finally, a memorable signoff: "Please apologize for your stupidity. There are a many thank you."[47]

There are 1.2 billion people learning a foreign language on any given day, all over the world.[48] And Luis knew that this number encompasses a population far greater than students "commay-tallay-vous-ing" their way through high school French classes. In the United States alone, there are over five million people who have spent more than $500 dollars on foreign language lesson software.[49] Using what he'd learned from creating CAPTCHA and how he'd been able to translate ten seconds of human energy into the digitizing power of reCAPTCHA, Luis created Duolingo. Duolingo is a free online language learning platform that also serves as a crowd-sourced text translation system. Duolingo was born because Luis was able to connect the dots in technology, culture, language and information in a way that no one had before.

The techniques that Duolingo uses to teach language are both unique and successful because of the way that he is able to use and parse data. The user interface is designed as a game that is engaging and fun to play, but the pedagogy is a real breakthrough.

As Luis explained, "We looked at the different theories of language pedagogy when we started out, and we discovered that they're like diets: There are thousands of them, they're not well supported by data, and they all contradict one another."[50]

Working at the scale of millions gives him the advantage of being able to engineer better teaching methods. "For example, we might look at our data and see that a lot of people are having trouble learning how adjectives work. So we posit that maybe we should teach adverbs before we teach adjectives. We try that approach on the next 25,000 people and compare the results with those for a control group of equivalent size; if the data show that it works better, we adapt the system to incorporate the new pedagogy."[51]

Everything Luis does is based on data generated from large sets of learners. "You can't engineer this kind of systematic improvement working with a classroom of thirty-five or fifty people. This is really the first time in history that you can bring together huge numbers of people, rigorously observe and compare minute differences that improve their ability to learn, and then combine all those improvements to create something much better."[52]

Language pedagogies are like diets. They have questionable efficacy and all disagree. Learning at the scale of millions, we can now use data and engineering to dramatically improve pedagogy.

For people who grow up in developing countries like Luis's native Guatemala, Duolingo is more than a hobby, it's a boot-strapping tool. As Luis explained, "[T]he majority of people in the world who want to learn a language are learning English because it might get them a better job." And these people don't have money to spend on language lessons. Luis's challenge was how to make Duolingo free and keep it that way. The solution came in a way analogous to his breakthrough with reCAPTCHA. In that problem, he took the online work people were doing to verify that they were human and reused it to digitize books. In Duolingo, Luis takes the online work people are doing learning a new language and reuses it to perform the service of translating content on websites.

More specifically, in Duolingo, when learners reach a certain level, the sentences they practice on are actual sentences from news websites that need translation. When enough people get the same translation, the system considers it accurately translated and uses it. Done at scale, this method of translating basic website content is as accurate as using professional translators. One example stunningly illustrates how accurately Duolingo's users translated a sample text from German:

Sample input (German): *Falls Pakistans Geschichte ein Indikator ist, so könnte Musharrafs Entscheidung, das Kriegsrecht zu verhängen, jener sprichwörtliche Tropfen sein, der das Fass zum Überlaufen bringt.*

Professional translator (at the cost of 20 cents a word): If Pakistan's history is *any* indicator, Musharraf's decision to impose martial law *may prove to be* the proverbial straw that breaks the camel's back.

Duolingo: If Pakistan's history is *an* indicator, Musharraf's decision to impose martial law *could be* the proverbial straw that breaks the camel's back.[53]

It works for the same reason reCAPTCHA works. When the same answer is given many times by people working individually, a useable translation of straightforward text is yielded. (Note that this method of translation fails on highly complex, nuanced and subjective texts, such as poetry.) It's also successful because there is a fun motivation factor built in: Duolingo works with real content, from sites like the *New York Times,* CNN, *Buzzfeed* and PBS.[54] So for many students, the content is more engaging, current and relevant than many of the made-up translation exercises in outdated language textbooks.

When Duolingo debuted, Apple named it "iPhone app of the year," pushing the number of users a week to a reported 20 million. A quarter of Duolingo's "players" live in North America; a larger percentage (35 percent) lives in Latin America. For Luis von Ahn, the benefits are multiple: he uses science and engineering to solve several major needs he's passionate about—learning languages, web translation and bringing people together by enabling them to communicate without language as a barrier. And he's found a sustainable economic model to support his commitment that learning languages should be free.

He has done so much; it's hard to remember that Luis von Ahn is now just thirty-five years old. He is excited about the potential for building systems that combine millions of learners with technology to tackle previously unsolvable problems. This method exudes possibility. Might it work in aspects of health care? For example, would it be a feasible project for radiology, for example, in which there are interns and residents reading X-rays of patients in remote parts of the world? Alternatively, could this model be used for programming, teaching people how to write code, or perhaps in work related to computer system security? Luis's hope is that people will look at his platform and business model and figure out how to apply them to many other areas. For Luis, the important thing is "getting capabilities to large numbers of people who need them—for free—and having a sustainable business model behind that whose monetization strategy is neither exploitive nor is it charity."[55]

8

THE POWER OF
DIFFERENCE

ONE OF THE THINGS THAT MAKES CONNECTIONAL INTEL-
ligence such a force for good is that it allows people to come together,
without sacrificing what makes them unique. In other words, this chapter is about the connectional intelligence of freaks, geeks and other
proud outsiders.

Pharrell Williams was never your typical rapper. He grew up in
Virginia Beach; his Mom was a teacher, his Dad was a handyman. In
school, he wasn't the cool guy. He met his producing partner, Chad
Hugo, during seventh grade band camp. Chad played the tenor saxo-
phone and Pharrell played keyboards and drums. The two band-nerd
friends formed a group called the Neptunes, which they imagined as a
modern day incarnation of old-school Motown guy groups like Smokey
Robinson and the Miracles, or The Temptations. From the beginning,
Pharrell's high-pitched falsetto was one of his most distinctive musical
traits. By the time he and Chad graduated high school, the Neptunes
were signed with top producer Ted Riley.

Connectional intelligence allows people to come together,
while standing strong in what makes them unique.

But in the 1990s, rap ruled, and the Neptunes soon found success writing and producing songs like Wreckx-n-Effect "Rump Shaker" and Nelly's "Hot in Herre." By August 2003, Pharrell and the Neptunes had produced a stunning 20 percent of all the music being played on British pop radio and 43 percent of the music being played on American pop stations.[1] It seemed Pharrell had that rare gift for creating music—tracks, hooks and lyrics—that was always one step ahead of the curve. Then, in 2006, he released his first solo single, "In My Mind," and the album tanked. For Pharrell, the failure of the first album on which he'd fully fronted his own work was devastating. It took him a long time to see the reason behind it: he wasn't being true to himself. He remembers that he was trying to "be like my peers—the Jays and the Puffs of the world, who make great music. But their purposes and their intentions are just completely different than what I have discovered in myself."[2]

He took a step back and asked himself how could his music serve a higher purpose, "because I felt like I had amassed this big body of work, most—not all—but most of which was just about self-aggrandizement, and I wasn't proud of it. So I couldn't be proud of the money that I had; I couldn't be proud of all the stuff that I had. I was thankful, but what did it mean? What did I do?"[3]

What he did was harken back to who he was as a kid in Virginia Beach, when he played in the marching band after school and spent hours on the weekends at the local skate park. He realized he'd never felt fully at home in the world of hardcore hip-hop, he was tired of trying to mimic the titans of that world—Jay Z, P. Diddy. He took his wealth, time and his energy and created "i am OTHER," an organization dedicated to reaching young people who feel different and helping them use their unique talents to launch creative ventures. As Pharrell states in the organization's mission statement, "We are proud to be different and believe that individuality is the new wealth. This shared philosophy flows through each pillar within our organization: music, film, television, apparel, tech and multimedia."[4] There's a friendship behind Pharrell's public success that harkens back to many connectionally intelligent friendships and partnerships throughout history.

For example, Albert Einstein referred to his closest friend, Michele Besso, as "the best sounding board in Europe."[5] It was through their daily walks, a shared love of the violin and scientific exchange that Einstein was able to create his theory of relativity. As Einstein recalled at a lecture in Kyoto in 1922:

> That was a very beautiful day when I visited him [Besso] and began to talk with him as follows: "I have recently had a question which was difficult for me to understand. So I came here today to bring with me a battle on the question." Trying a lot of discussions with him, I could suddenly comprehend the matter. Next day I visited him again and said to him without greeting "Thank you. I've completely solved the problem."[6]

In his book *Powers of Two,* Joshua Shenk explores the lives and accomplishments of scores of creative duos. Shenk shows that the romantic myth of the lone genius fails because it obscures the social, connected qualities of innovation.[7] Shenk goes on to claim that the pair is a "primary creative unit," because it can be seen in case after case as a fundamental, fractal, and recurring shape in the patterns of innovation.[8] We agree: the creative pair is a natural and powerful expression of connectional intelligence that is often central to getting big things done.

When Pharrell decided to reboot not only his career, but his entire approach to the music industry, and to focus on service and giving a voice to kids who were like himself, he turned to his close friend Mimi Valdes, the former editor-in-chief of *Vibe* and *Latina* magazines. Pharrell, who had long leaned on Valdes' advice, asked her to join i am OTHER as creative director, not only to be his sounding board but also to bring to his many ventures her own mix of innovation and fierce integrity. "I was unsure at first," she admitted. "I had never done this before. But I had to check myself—I *have* done this before. I know how to create content, and this is just a different form of content. Also, I know more than anybody how to help Pharrell execute his vision."[9]

At i am OTHER, Pharrell funded and mentored kids who wanted to break into all of the fields to which he had access: fashion and entertainment, but also tech and manufacturing. He drew on the talent and creativity of the young people who had grown up on his music to start Bionic Yarn and other initiatives. Bionic Yarn, which creates textiles from recycled plastic bottles, has been tremendously successful, inking partnerships with companies like Kiehls, Cole Haan and the Gap.

He also created the Collaborative Fund, a venture capitalist fund that he described as "an investment fund focused on supporting and investing in the shared future. The fund centers around two macro themes which we believe to be at the core of business innovation in the coming years: the growth of the creative class and the collaborative economy."[10] The investor team for the Collaborative Fund includes Chad Hurley, co-founder of YouTube; Chuck Temple, founder of OpenTable; Jessica Jackley, co-founder of Kiva; and Tony Hsieh, CEO of Zappos. In addition to funding creative new companies, the Collaborative Fund has also funded innovative projects from the team at Sesame Street and Children's Television Workshop.[11]

Inspired by his success, Pharrell did more—he co-founded a manufacturing company, Brooklyn Machine Works, that crafts handmade bikes. And he founded From One Hand to anOther, which has brought

STEM (Science, Technology, Engineering and Mathematics) curriculum to underserved kids in communities across the country.

He was so busy and so satisfied and felt so fully himself that what he really needed to do, what he wanted to do, he said, was get back into the studio and make music again. The result was "Happy," an unabashedly joyful song that went on to become the greatest hit of Pharrell's career, selling millions of copies. Its 24-hour video, 24hoursofhappiness.com, reinvented and reinvigorated the music video format. And then the United Nations called. They wanted to partner with Pharrell to promote the International Day of Happiness on March 20, 2014. All around the world, people submitted videos of themselves—singing and dancing, serenading their loved ones, dancing with children, family, pets and friends. For Pharrell, who discovered, literally, a world of connection through embracing his otherness, this has been more than the biggest spike of his career. As he put it, it's the discovery of his life's work. "I didn't know what my path was. I knew that I was meant to do something different. I knew that I needed to inject purpose in my music." He called everything that led to his greatest failure, "just training." Now when he considers any decision, creative or otherwise, he tells himself, "keep putting purpose in everything you do. Don't worry about it; just put purpose in there."[12]

Productivity, innovation and job satisfaction
all rise when people connect and share what's
true to them and their essential gifts.

Covering is a concept coined by sociologist Erving Goffman and expanded many decades later by New York University law professor Kenji Yoshino. Covering is "to tone down a disfavored identity to fit into the mainstream," Yoshino suggests.[13] As a musical artist, Pharrell was in a field where it was relatively easy to be his authentic self, once he discovered what that was. In the corporate world, this is far more challenging. And it's more than a matter of pure self-expression. The problem with covering is that, in the corporate world, most individuals believe that they can't bring their authentic selves to work. In cultures where employees feel they must cover, companies aren't getting everything they can from the people who work for them.

Christie Smith, the national managing principal for the Deloitte University Leadership Center for Inclusion, realized what a critical error this was for business—and decided to do something about it. Recognizing covering as an obstacle that stunts employees and impacts organizational growth, she did more research on the dimensions of Yoshino's covering concept. Yoshino believes that four different ways of covering typically manifest within corporate culture: appearance-based, affiliation-based, advocacy-based and association-based.

Christie connected with Yoshino and suggested they work together to understand covering in the corporate environment. They surveyed more than 3,000 employees in organizations spanning ten different industries. The survey revealed that 83 percent of lesbian, gay and bisexual (LGB) individuals, 79 percent of Blacks, 67 percent of women of color, 66 percent of women, 63 percent of those identifying as Hispanic/Latino and 45 percent of heterosexual white men cover at work. Not surprisingly, 53 percent of respondents said they believed the leaders of their organizations expect them to cover. A majority of the participants felt that if they didn't cover, they wouldn't fit in to their company's culture and consequently wouldn't succeed.

So how did Christie get her own Deloitte employees to acknowledge and celebrate what makes them different? First, she worked with fifty senior Deloitte leaders to model the ideal of uncovering. They launched an internal campaign called "Share Your Story" in which the fifty leaders discussed bringing their authentic selves to work in a series of short videos. For example, directors Neil Neveras and Kevin Walker, a gay couple, shared their story. They spoke about how their different perspective enabled them to build deeper connections with many different kinds of people, from co-workers to clients. Deloitte's Chief Inclusion Officer Deborah DeHaas shared how her mother, a pioneer in the accounting field, inspired her to reach for the top and instilled in her the values she champions today. Other stories told of personal struggles with issues like illness, family, doubts, ambition and purpose.[14]

The campaign was well received; it showed, anecdotally, that when leaders uncover, employees across the organization feel more inclined to do so as well. Deloitte has approximately 65,000 US professionals—the "trickle down" effect of the Share Your Story campaign could touch thousands of client teams.[15] Imagine working in a connected environment where sharing your stories is part of what makes your organization strong. The empathy is palpable.

Christie Smith and Kenji Yoshino's study *Uncovering Talent* is based on the premise that productivity, innovation and job satisfaction all rise when people connect and share what's true to them and to their essential gifts. Christie's external connections brought the powerful idea into Deloitte. She leveraged many different internal groups to move the concept to the center of the organization and to help build profound connections, regardless of rank, expertise and functional role.

Not content to stop at Deloitte's borders, she is now bringing this work to the world by mobilizing her team to create and launch a diagnostic tool with which other organizations can close the gap between a professed value for diversity and inclusion and actual practices. Christie found the idea of covering, which was developed for civil rights policy, and connected covering to business and leadership and asked: What is the cost to corporations of covering? What if it could be different for all employees? She had the insight to understand that uncovering can spark connectional intelligence. The takeaway is that we can all ask ourselves: What's true about me that I feel I have to cover or hide? What if I could share that in a way that lets me be more connected and, therefore, more able to bring all of my talents to my organization?

For many Muslim women a physical covering is a symbol of religious faith. In certain sects, a Muslim woman must be covered all the time. The full burqa. Body covered head to foot. Even if she wants to go for a swim.

Aheda Zanetti was only a baby when her family migrated to Australia. If you hear audio of her speaking, without looking at her image, she sounds a lot like Australian actress Toni Collette. The two women, both in their early forties, grew up in Sydney at the same time. They might have gone to the same schools, frequented the same movie theaters and shopping centers and passed each other on the street dozens of times.

When Aheda arrived in Australia, the country was still in the throes of what was called the "The Ten Pound Pom," a migration program that the nation had adopted after World War II. Fearing invasion from Japan, and aware that Australia's sparsely populated country had a vastly underdeveloped economy, the government came up with a "Populate or Perish" scheme. For ten pounds, adults could gain passage to Australia, and their children could travel for free. But a preexisting "White Australia" policy restricted almost all immigration to whites from Europe, favoring those from Great Britain. (Pom is Aussie slang for an Englishman.)

Because the government had taken pains to keep the door closed to those who were different from them, traditionally clothed Muslims were still a rarity in Australia when Aheda was growing up. The "White Australia" policy was not completely abolished until 1978, when Aheda was halfway through primary school. But the policy, having been upheld by the Australian government for more than seventy-five years, cast a long shadow on the make-up of the Australian citizenship and shaped how race would frame opportunity and hierarchy in the country for decades to come.

Aheda was a stay-at-home mother of three when she invented the burqini. She had grown up in a Muslim family where women were not only modest, they were largely sedentary. Aheda and her mom friends often discussed what they had missed out on as children and what they hoped would be different for their own children. One afternoon, she took her children to see her niece play netball, and as she remembered it, "I saw my niece playing in this match. She was the only one veiled."[16] Aheda remembered feeling both proud of her niece for embracing her athleticism, but also sympathetic to the fact that the girl was literally sweltering under her covering. "I looked at her and her face was so red, red, red, in her uniform," she said. "So I got my fabrics and my creative mind and I asked myself, 'What would I wear if I was playing football? What would I wear if I was playing netball?' So it was a design that was created through the thoughts of me, 'How would *I* feel comfortable?'"[17]

Aheda also felt strongly that her active wear designs should be adaptable to the Western lifestyle. "The symbol of the veil, with excess fabrics and tucking, did not suit me at all in regards to a sports garment," she said. "I wanted it to be adaptable with Western culture."[18]

The first design she created was what she called a "hijood"—an undergarment that was part rash guard, with a hood that a teenage girl could comfortably wear underneath a school sports jersey. "She could do handstands and cartwheels," Aheda says. "Because there's no excess fabric. The fabric is totally breathable, it's got the sweat wicking and it's got all the ingredients to make you feel comfortable."[19]

The burqini was a swimwear adaptation of the hijood. Aheda tested fabric samples from all over the world. She knew that Muslim women wore extra veils to cover the chest area to preserve modesty in the front. So she created prints with transfers and material that was thick enough that it did the modesty work of the veil. Aheda remembers it was "more about the mind work than the actual visual design. We wanted a Muslim woman to feel *very* comfortable wearing it because the goal was to encourage healthy lifestyles."[20]

Aheda came up with the term "burqini" because early prototypes of her product were being marketed as "an Islamic swimsuit." She had grown up being "the other" her whole life. She didn't want this product, which would allow Muslim women in Australia to fully participate in the outdoor life and beach culture that is so much a part of the national identity, to feel that the very name of what they wore highlighted their difference.

In 2005, the legacy of "White Australia" reared its ugly head when riots between white and Lebanese Australian youth raged into the night. Fueled by alcohol and a long-brewing mistrust between the two groups, more than 5,000 young people crowded the beach as police struggled to contain the violence.[21] Property damage and beatings claimed victims of every color. The aftermath was so grave that Great Britain, Canada and Indonesia issued travel warnings, urging their citizens to avoid non-essential travel to Australia.[22]

One local Muslim citizen told the media, "We knew always there was racism, but we never knew it was to this extent. I mean, all your life you've been—you've been raised to be Australian. I mean, you carry the Australian flag. When you go to sports events and all that, you're happy to be Australian and all that. And all of sudden people reject you. 'Go home!' They shout your names. Like, 'Go home, you Middle Eastern Lebs,' or whatever. 'Go home.' I mean, that's a shock to us. 'Go home.' I mean, like, you get cut inside your heart, you know. Like you feel like you're not part of society no more."[23]

In the wake of the riots, numerous efforts were made to embrace the multiculturalism that was threatening to tear the nation apart. Religious progressives of different backgrounds formed an organization called "Common Dreams," which met with much success. Because the beach is a symbolic and central part of the national identity, the government funded an initiative called "On the Same Wave." The program, administered by Surf Life Saving Australia, actively sought to recruit young Muslims to be trained as life guards, helping them to earn a natural place in and on the beaches of Australia. A young woman named Mecca Laalaa was the first Muslim woman to be certified by the "On the Same Wave" program—she wore a custom-made burqini in the red and yellow colors of Surf Life Saving Australia. The colors were instantly recognizable to young people across the country and carried the same weight as the colors of the Los Angeles Lakers or the Miami Heat might do in the United States. A photo of Laalaa went viral in the Australian media and then around the world. Orders for the burqini exploded. The Australian Trade Commission would later credit Laalaa and her designer Aheda with restoring the cultural integrity of Australia's international reputation that had been so damaged by the riots. In 2011, the Macquarie Dictionary (the Australian equivalent of Webster's) named "burqini" their word of the year.

Today, the burqini's impact has gone way beyond Aheda's goal of creating garments that would allow Australian Muslim women to pursue an active lifestyle. In fact, 30 percent of the women who buy burqinis buy them not for reasons of religious modesty, but for health reasons.[24] Burqinis are worn by women who want to swim after having survived disfigurements caused by cancer and other life threatening illnesses. They are worn by women whose skin has been made ultra-sensitive to the sun by necessary and life-saving medicines. And they are worn by women of diverse body types who are determined to be active and just don't want to be exposed (Aheda now makes a version with a removable head-covering).

Aheda's burqini shows the power of what Frans Johansson calls the "Medici Effect," which occurs when disparate ideas are brought together.[25] In today's connected world, women determined to be active despite their situations—women with different needs and essentially the same solution—can find each other, understand each other and act.

Pat Mitchell was always known as a "connector." The former CEO of PBS and the current president of the Paley Center for Media, Pat's media fame includes a lifetime of work as a reporter, news anchor, talk show host, White House and special correspondent, producer and executive. Her documentaries and specials have received thirty-seven Emmy Awards, five Peabody Awards and two Academy Award nominations.

Connection was how she got her job done. Who you knew translated very much into what you knew. "The first third of my life, connections were essential to get from where I was, a young girl with big dreams in the deep rural South with no money, no influence, no connections," Pat explains. "The second third of my life as a reporter and journalist, you are only as good as your contacts. I learned very quickly as a young journalist that everything was about connections; that's how you got a story, understood the story, and communicated the story. It began with who your contacts were and how strong your connections were. You learned to keep in touch; to cultivate contacts, to strengthen connections." Now, she thinks about connection more in terms of life as much as work. "My connections are much more about who I want to know, be friends with, spend time with and who enhances my life in some meaningful way, the pleasure of knowing people and through them, experiencing the power of sharing."[26]

After attending a few TED conferences, she and her husband had dinner with her friend, Jacqueline Novogratz, founder of Acumen, and her husband, Chris Anderson, TED's curator and owner. The conversation turned to the behind-the-scenes operation of TED, specifically how speakers were selected. Pat had noticed at that time fewer women speakers than men at TED, and in mentioning this, learned that TED looked for great TEDTalks from women, and sometimes, after extending invitations, the women would cancel with reasons ranging from schedule challenges to deferring to male colleagues. Pat had heard this before in curating other women's conferences.[27]

This troubled her, for if there was one truth Pat Mitchell had discovered during her distinguished career in media, it was that there is no shortage of talented women with ideas worth sharing. She told the TED team she was willing to suggest some. Given the invitation, she followed up and got to know the TED curating team.

Together with the small group of TED women team leaders, she explored an idea: a TED conference focusing on and celebrating women, co-sponsored with the Paley Center. To make this work, forming a partnership with the internal women at TED was critical; specifically June Cohen, TED's media director; Ronda Carnegie, TED's corporate partnership lead; and Lara Stein, then the TEDx coordinator. They became advocates and formed the internal TEDWomen team. The first TEDWomen conference was held in Washington in 2010.

Mitchell's vision, and her warm, transparent sense of purpose to build a new TED community in full partnership with TED's women team, brought distinguished luminaries, including Hillary Clinton, Madeleine Albright and Nancy Pelosi, as well as 67 more women speakers and 19 men.

TEDWomen was the result of Pat's long-honed connectional intelligence and collaborative teamwork. She knew how to tap into her vast networks of people. She had, over decades, developed the emotional intelligence to imbue those networks with meaning. The TED conference model had already laid the groundwork in technology—using the enormous digital modals that bring people, powerful ideas and historical knowledge together in an unprecedented way.

The first TEDWomen conference spawned hundreds of TEDx Women gatherings, some in countries as far away as Saudi Arabia and Mongolia, creating a global conversation with TEDx organizers taking the live feed of TEDWomen and hosting and curating talks by the outstanding women (and men) in their communities. To Pat Mitchell's network were added many others; a global community of organizers for TEDxWomen events and a virtual community that included everything from undergraduate campuses to corporate offices to local chapters. In the United States, one impact of the success of TEDWomen and TEDxWomen, and the new communities these conferences attracted, has been more women attending and speaking at TED and TEDGlobal.

> *When you get big things done using connectional intelligence, there is a ripple effect. You accomplish many things, including things you could not have imagined when you began.*

By creating new forums, opening new channels, connecting, and amplifying, Pat and the internal TEDWomen team achieved the original goal of presenting the TED audience with more women who had ideas worth sharing. The fact that TEDWomen was such a success would alone have made it a powerful example of getting big things done. But connectional intelligence is fluid and adaptive. What you've seen, again and again in this book, are examples that echo Pat's. When you get big things done using connectional intelligence, there is a ripple effect. You not only accomplish one goal, in the process, you accomplish many things: including things you could not have imagined when you began.

In digital media, there is constant talk of rapid growth—of "scaling." Pat Mitchell's idea scaled. "Many connections have been made at TEDWomen, some of which have been life-changing for the speakers and attendees," she reports. "That's the biggest reward, knowing that a young Afghan woman courageously running a girls school in Kabul has had dozens of volunteers coming from the United States and Europe to teach and mentor because they heard her TEDWomen talk. TEDWomen was the place where Sheryl Sandberg 'leaned in' and gave the talk that became a global book bestseller and movement; where a husband and wife shared the personal story behind their new Internet business, and it was sold when their talk went live on TED.com. So many important connections are made at every TED. It's one of the key components to the experience, along with the connections that come from the ideas heard and shared."[28]

TEDxWomen offers a world where people can choose to connect across race, economic status, nationality and geography. Sometimes, the decision is thrust upon them.

Anyone who has ever lived with or loved someone with a life-threatening illness knows that disease thrusts you into another world where—despite your race, your economic status, your nationality—you are immediately an "other." As Susan Sontag wrote so powerfully, "Illness is the night side of life, a more onerous citizenship. Everyone who is born holds dual citizenship, in the kingdom of the well and in the kingdom of the sick. Although we all prefer to use the good passport, sooner or later each of us is obliged, at least for a spell, to identify ourselves as citizens of that other place."[29]

In *The Fault in Our Stars,* a teenaged girl afflicted with a fatal cancer tries not to fall in love with a boy who has a less fatal cancer because she doesn't want him to be hurt when she dies. That's anything but a common plot in young adult (YA) fiction: before the novel was published, author John Green said he'd sign every copy that was pre-ordered. He had no idea he'd be signing 150,000 copies. Or that *Time* magazine would call his novel for teenagers the best young adult fiction of the year. Or that *Fault* would sell a million copies and become a movie.

John Green is now a magic name in YA fiction, but he's been a hugely influential figure for a long time online and in the community of millions of teen readers. In 2007, he and his brother Hank—founder of EcoGeek, an environmental/technology blog—decided not to talk to each other for a year. Instead, they communicated on videoblogs posted every weekday on YouTube. They called their project Brotherhood 2.0. Their hopes were modest: "When we started making videos we hoped that we'd build a small but active community of viewers who would join us in projects."[30] Small but active is what they got: 10,000 participants.

Many of these participants called themselves "Nerdfighters." John calls them "people who care more than other people." A dictionary of online slang is more poetic, defining "Nerdfighters" as "people who in-stead of being made up of cells and organs and stuff are actually made out of awesome."[31] By any definition, their first mission is blunt and eloquent: to "increase awesome and decrease suck" in the world. Their second mission is just as direct: to create a community for kids who can't quite pass for normal.

Brotherhood 2.0 became Nerdfighters. And the Green brothers kept on videoblogging. They attracted a community of gays, transgen-der kids, teens with diseases, victims of bullies and just plain smart and sensitive teens—more than a million members. (It's easy to become a member: "If you want to be a Nerdfighter, you are a Nerdfighter."[32]) John Green says, "We don't really want Nerdfighters to be a mainstream cultural phenomenon. I worry that mainstream cultural phenomena need, like, Message Singularity and A Brand and an Institutional Voice and stuff. That kind of thing does not interest us at all. We just want to make cool stuff with people we like."[33]

"Cool stuff" means projects like the Kiva.org Lending Team that Nerdfighters launched in 2008. Six years later, the Kiva Nerdfighters group ranks eighth on the Kiva site, and the 44,000 Kiva Nerdfighter members have made microloans of $3.6 million. Nerdfighters have also donated to World Vision, Save the Children and The Uncultured Project; once a year, they stage the Project for Awesome, which helps hundreds of charities.

"Decrease world suck," "DFTBA" ("Don't Forget To Be Awesome") and other Nerdfighter phrases can be found on many commercial products. There's a Kate Spade wallet, an Urban Outfitters rug, a Hobby Lobby poster, a Delia's T-shirt. If John Green were to trademark these terms, he could collect millions from these companies. But he won't trademark, even though he knows that his intellectual property has been infringed. For John, the Nerdfighters is primarily a community defined by its shared values and ideas.

John Green created an empathic playground for over a million subscribers of freaks, geeks and other proud outsiders.

Esther Earl, a Nerdfighter who had cancer, was John Green's inspiration for *The Fault in Our Stars*. She died before the novel was published. But Esther wasn't forgotten. John dedicated the book to her. And in a videoblog, he introduced a new phrase: "Rest in awesome."[34] No Nerdfighter who saw it failed to grasp that John had lived up to the Nerdfighter creed—"Know that you'll always have a whole community of nerdfighting friends to support you"[35]—straight into the afterlife.

John Green used his connectional intelligence to create an empathic playground where young people could express what they really felt. Because they rallied around it and had access to the tools to connect, Nerdfighters happened. Today, it's home for over a million subscribers of freaks, geeks and other proud outsiders.

WHY NOT?

Reimagining What's Possible

THE ASTONISHING POWER OF CONNECTIONAL INTELLI-gence to get big things done can be found even in the unlikely world of people with crippling rare diseases. In 1962, Jeannie was a four-year-old girl living in Michigan when the Mayo Clinic diagnosed her with *fibro-dysplasia ossificans progressiva,* or FOP. The medical community classifies FOP as an orphan disease, one that's so rare that treatments are limited, if not nonexistent. FOP caused Jeannie to grow entirely new bones from stem cells. These bones attach to her original bones, eventually making movement impossible.[1] The little girl whose bruises turned into jutting bones was actually growing a second skeleton. Eventually she would be locked in her body by a cage of her own bones and die. And there was nothing doctors could do. They did not expect her to live long enough to graduate from high school. Jeannie's parents were told to take her home, love her and enjoy her for as long as she lived.[2]

More than fifty years later, Jeannie Peeper has defied every one of those early predictions. It is not that the disease hasn't performed the way doctors said it would. When Jeannie turned sixteen, she could drive, and then she couldn't. She could dress herself, and then she couldn't. Now she's confined to a wheelchair and has very limited movement. No medicine has been invented to ease Jeannie's suffering or slow down the onset of her symptoms. And yet, she has not only single-handedly rewritten the case book for FOP by her own statistically long and active life, she has made sure that FOP is no longer an orphan disease, by building a network of patients, doctors and researchers who have made FOP their life's work.

In her early twenties, a fall necessitated full-time care, so her parents urged her to move from Michigan to Florida, where they had recently retired. There, she attended the University of Central Florida, where she earned a degree in social work and successfully completed internships in nursing homes and rehabilitation centers. Jeannie graduated college, a significant accomplishment for a person dealing with the challenges of FOP. Then, just a few weeks after graduation, another fall caused more new bones to grow, and even more limited mobility. Jeannie realized that her dream of getting a job as a social worker would be almost impossible if she couldn't even get dressed by herself.[3]

By using connectional intelligence to build a network of patients, doctors and researchers, Jeannie Peeper transformed the research about and treatment of her rare disease.

Feeling isolated, angry, alone and depressed, Jeannie began to look for answers. Her doctors back in Michigan referred her to a National Institutes of Health physician named Michael Zasloff. It was a moment of connection that would spark a revolution in FOP. Unlike most doctors Jeannie had met, Zasloff had seen another case of FOP early in his career as a surgical intern. When he went to other doctors to ask for answers about FOP, they were frank with him: they had no idea what caused it and had no idea how to treat it. Zasloff, almost a decade before he met Jeannie, began doing research. He realized that while FOP had been documented as early as 1736, only two research papers had been written on FOP in the *entire* twentieth century. In the ten years between his first FOP patient and his meeting Jeannie, Zasloff had found and examined an additional eighteen patients. It doesn't sound like much, but this is the thing about connectional intelligence: sometimes the numbers don't have to be staggering for us to get big things done. Sometimes, a small, focused effort over a long time can change the world in some significant way. By caring for eighteen patients with FOP, Zasloff had quietly made himself one of the leading authorities in the disease. What Jeannie did with those eighteen names is nothing short of extraordinary.

First she sent a letter and questionnaire to every patient on the list. In the years since he had met them, some of Zasloff's patients had died, but all eleven of the surviving patients wrote Jeannie back. Despite her limited movement, over the next year Jeannie went to see some of the surviving patients in person. She saw these men, women and children as more than fellow patients, she saw them as the building blocks of an army that would take FOP down. She wanted to see them in person, get to know them, make it clear that she would be relentless on their behalf.[4] Jeannie began a newsletter, which she put out four times a year called "FOP Connection." Then, with those eleven other patients, she started what she boldly called the International Fibrodysplasia Ossificans Progressiva Association (IFOPA). Together, the group began compiling data and recruiting doctors to look at all the ways that FOP manifests itself.[5]

It turns out that it doesn't take a ton of cash to save a rare disease from being orphaned by the medical community. One family Jeannie connected with raised $30,000 in a golf tournament. Other families hosted Bingo nights and barbecues, ice-fishing tournaments and swim-a-thons. In 2012, the IFOPA raised more than half a million dollars. That's lemonade stand money compared to the one billion dollars a year that the National Institutes of Health designates for diabetes research, but it turns out that it's enough to move the needle from hopeless to miraculous. Along with other donations and university grants, Jeannie was able to assemble a small team headed by a physician and a geneticist whose sole mission is to study and innovate treatment, care and prevention of FOP.[6]

And this is where one woman on a mission has, unexpectedly, become not only the center of groundbreaking research about the disease that has haunted and defined her life, but the center of a much bigger conversation about something that affects us all. For patients with FOP, every new bone that grows is pure punishment, causing a domino effect of health problems, the least of which is living within a body that fossilizes itself with every new bump and bruise. But, as Jeannie's team of physicians and researchers discovered, the ability to create brand new healthy bones is actually an amazing thing. What they are learning about FOP has a host of applications in the mainstream medical community: from how to help bones repair after fractures to how to combat the lower bone density that affects more than 61 percent of women and 38 percent of men after the age of fifty.[7]

The work Jeannie Peeper has begun will, likely, not affect her much in the span of her lifetime. But because she connected the dots, selflessly and tirelessly, she has already improved the quality of life for a generation of young people living with FOP. Doctors no longer tell the parents of four-year-olds diagnosed with the disease to "love the child as long as you can because she will not live long." They tell them what the pitfalls are, they warn them against surgeries and procedures that can make the illness accelerate, and they tell them to contact Jeannie

Peeper and her team of miracle workers. It *is* a rare disease, they say, but you are not alone.

Many patients with rare diseases spend years going from doctor to doctor playing a medical version of the old game show, *Name That Tune*. Misdiagnosis is common, not because doctors aren't informed and on top of the research, but because it would be impossible for any one doctor to keep track of seven thousand rare diseases, especially since hundreds of new rare diseases are discovered each year.

CrowdMed is an online medical crowd-sourcing platform on which people submit medical cases with information about symptoms, medical history, family history and other relevant data. Then a community of "medical detectives" suggests diagnoses and places bets on the outcomes they think are most likely. As CrowdMed has discovered, the majority of their "medical detectives" are active in medicine, but people outside of medicine participate as well. CrowdMed uses market algorithms to aggregate the information from the community and distill it down to a probable list of diagnostic suggestions for each patient.

CrowdMed is the brainchild of Jared Heyman, who watched a lack of diagnosis almost kill his little sister. One day, Carly Heyman was a bright and enthusiastic college freshman. She was eighteen years old, but she swore she was having the kind of hot flashes most commonly exhibited in menopausal women. She slept at night with water bottles because she'd wake up with night terrors, covered with sweat. Carly dropped out of college and moved back in with her parents. No doctor could offer a satisfying diagnosis. Three years later, Carly's mother spent every night sleeping in her daughter's bed. Carly's night terrors had increased, but so had her depression. She was afraid that alone, in the middle of the night, faced with the kind of agony doctors couldn't diagnosis or remedy, she might try to commit suicide. After three long years, Carly's doctors diagnosed her with *fragile X-associated primary ovarian insufficiency*. It is a rare disease, but the treatment is straightforward:

hormone replacement therapy. Within three weeks, almost all of Carly's symptoms were gone.[8]

While his sister struggled to put a name to her odd assortment of symptoms, Jared Heyman was living in Atlanta, where he ran an online survey company. At that company, he learned all about the wisdom of crowds. He believed that "a large group of nonexperts can be very wise once you have the right mechanisms in place to aggregate their collective intelligence."[9] It is all about designing the right type of questions.

You don't need a medical degree—or any degree—to join Crowd-Med. Indeed, it's set up like a game; when you start, you get "points" that you can use to bet on a diagnosis. Solutions are like stocks in the financial markets; they rise or fall, based on support from participants. The point of CrowdMed isn't to replace doctors: the idea is to give real patients potentially relevant information they can take back to their doctors, especially doctors who struggle to diagnose these rare diseases.

To get CrowdMed started, they ran tests with "mystery diseases." The results were encouraging. In twenty test cases, participants had high scores; 700 people included the mystery diseases in their top three diagnostic suggestions.

Patients pay CrowdMed a standard fee of $299, which is returned if the online crowd does not deliver a diagnosis that is either validated by the patient's doctor, or leads the doctor to a correct diagnosis. It sounds like a gamble, but it is one that many patients are willing to take. Jared believes his sister might have been spared years of pain and suffering if only CrowdMed had existed when she first began to experience symptoms of her disease. When Jared put forward all of Carly's symptoms as one of the site's first test cases, the crowd diagnosed her illness, correctly, in just three days.[10]

For years, scientific research was a specialized closed shop, especially in academic settings. Researchers spoke only to each other, using language no ordinary person could understand. Their work reached ever-narrower audiences, appearing only in professional journals that took several years and many peer reviews before they were approved for publication.

Dr. Eva Guinan, an associate professor at the Harvard Medical School, had a different idea. "If the guy next door can solve your problem for you," she said, "then by all means go next door, because it's efficient."[11] Dr. Guinan was not alone in calling for a frontal assault on traditional approaches to science. Dr. Karim Lakhani, an associate professor at Harvard Business School, had long been advocating crowd-sourcing—he called it "collecting information from untapped sources"—in a field where the idea of opening research to those "outside the walls" was unthinkable.

In 2010, Guinan, Lakhani and their associates created a cutting edge "ideas challenge" as their first foray into casting a wider net in the world of medical research. To make the idea challenge credible, they offered cash prizes of $2,500 apiece for ideas about Type 1 diabetes, once known as "juvenile diabetes" but also seen in adults. The disease can be managed by a patient's regular injection of the hormone insulin to make up for the body's inability to manufacture it, but in spite of active research no cure has yet been found.[12]

Drs. Guinan and Lakhani's goal was to see how many stages of research into Type 1 diabetes could benefit from openness in generating ideas, in evaluating them and in encouraging experts outside the field to join together and contribute. Drew Faust, president of Harvard University, sent out a mass e-mail to more than 250,000 people, everyone from janitors to deans, inviting them to participate in the idea challenge.

Equally nontraditional was the phrasing of the question the team asked. Because they believed that posing the right question might be more important than finding the right answer, theirs was an open-ended query: "What do we *not* know in order to cure Type 1 diabetes?"

"There are all these people out there," Dr. Guinan said. "They may teach nineteenth century English literature, but they're smart and motivated and their kids have diabetes. For years, they've had no place to ask the question: Why isn't somebody looking into this?"[13]

---

*A key question of the connectionally intelligent is not
"what do we know?" but "what do we not know?"*

The challenge was open for six weeks. The call for ideas attracted submissions from people from a broad spectrum of backgrounds, with only 9 percent of responders defining themselves as having "intimate knowledge of Type 1 diabetes research issues."[14] The suggestions of 779 respondents were winnowed down to 195 submissions. Twelve winners were chosen by averaging the opinions of a pool of 142 Harvard Medical School faculty—another unusual decision that took the results out of the hands of a small set of ten to fifteen senior experts in a peer review. Many of the top ideas came from participants who had a friend or relative with diabetes. What set the contest apart was that it put forward an important paradigm, one in which the questions were as valuable as the answers. The winners included Harvard staff members, with no scientific or medical background, as well as professors, research scientists, a retired dentist and a human resources professional with Type 1 diabetes. The contest revealed that patients, who had lived their whole lives with the disease, asked questions that the academic community had overlooked.

The project didn't stop there. Once the question-winners were selected, Guinan and Lakhani set out to form multidisciplinary teams to create larger combinations that might further the goal of attracting a more diverse set of researchers. They wanted to see if scientists from other life-science disciplines and disease specialties could potentially convert their research hypotheses into responsive experimental proposals in the Type 1 diabetes arena. In the end, seven proposals were funded by Harvard Medical School, five of which were led by principal investigators with no background of significant engagement in Type 1 diabetes research.[15]

Other leading health institutions including the U.S. National Institutes of Health, the Cleveland Clinic and the Juvenile Diabetes Research Foundation are now exploring how to build programs that mirror the open shop concept of the Harvard diabetes program.

Many of these stories are about individuals who combine asking powerful questions with maximizing their networks to get big things done. But sometimes this works in reverse. Asking questions to a huge number of people can lead you to unique and unexpected ideas or accomplishments. That's how it worked with MIT's massive open online course and a Mongolian student named Battushig Myanganbayar.

There may be more inhospitable climates than Mongolia, but not many. The summers are short. The winters are not just endless, but bitter; in January, morning temperatures can be as low as 40 degrees below zero. You might think that a small, mostly rural country would have clean air, but no—Mongolia has some of the worst pollution in the world.[16]

Battushig Myanganbayar grew up in Khan Uul, a neighborhood in Ulan Bator, where the average annual temperature is 27 degrees Fahrenheit. Play outside? Not for long. But that was not troubling for Battushig, who liked to tinker with machines and develop his electrical engineering skills. Battushig lived in a building in which the driveway had a blind-spot that made it unsafe for children playing outside. Worried about this ten-year-old sister and her friends, the fifteen-year-old student decided to do something about it. He tinkered with a sensor, a siren and a flashing red light and cobbled together a simple system that detected oncoming cars and flashed the siren to give his sister and the other children time to get out of the way when a car was coming.

Battushig was getting electronics training from some of the best: he was a sophomore-level student in MIT's online class in Circuits and Electronics. He took it not because it was offered by a prestigious university, but because the intro video for the massive open online version of the course promised that it would teach him to understand how iPhones work. He thought this alone was worth the time.[17]

He had the one great advantage that his country provides: For a decade, Mongolia has been building an extensive 3G network. Even in remote areas, homes without landlines generally have cell phones—and those phones operate at lightning speed.[18]

Battushig persuaded his parents to upgrade the Internet speed at their home from 1 megabit per second (mps) to 3 mps (the average in the United States is 8.6 mps) to make it easier to watch the MIT lectures. His methods of study were somewhat unusual: He watched two video lectures at the same time, simultaneously reading the subtitles on one of them while listening to the audio (in English) from the other.

He also did something else that few students take on: he produced his own lecture videos about the homework, in Mongolian, using You-Tube to help his classmates. "I developed my own technique to do minilectures by myself," Battushig explains.[19] He filmed himself by propping his iPhone on a bookshelf above his desk and videotaping as he worked out an equation on the page. As he worked he explained what he was doing aloud.

From an early age, it was obvious that Battushig was some kind of prodigy. But no one realized quite how exceptional he was until he scored 100 percent in the Circuits and Electronics class, something achieved by only 340 students out of 150,000.[20]

Battushig applied to the renowned Massachusetts Institute of Technology with support from his high school principal, Enkhmunkh Zurgaanjin, the first Mongolian to graduate from there. Battushig's perfect score made his acceptance a no-brainer from MIT's perspective.

The following year, he joined MIT's freshman class on campus in far-away Cambridge, Massachusetts. Today, in addition to his full load of scientific courses at MIT, Battushig is working with edX and the MIT Media Lab on improving the efficacy and reach of massive open online courses.

One of the oldest examples of connectional intelligence is the relationship between human beings and nature. We know that when we are tuned into the forces that surround us—our natural resources, the patterns of weather, animals, natural phenomena and disasters—we are able to achieve more than by pretending human beings live in a vacuum.

In 1850, noted English gardener and designer Joseph Paxton was inspired to design the Crystal Palace by considering the Victoria regla, a lily he'd carefully cultivated for the Duke of Devonshire.[21] The Victoria regla had never before been grown in England, because it was nearly impossible for the greenhouses to replicate the warm, swampy temperatures that made the lily thrive in the oxbow lakes and bayous of the Americas.

Inspired by the giant leaves of the lily, Joseph's blueprint for the Crystal Palace drew on the patterns of nature. He created transverse girders and supports that worked the same way the ribbed undersurface of the lily did in supporting its unusual weight and size. The result was the largest glass building ever.[22]

Joseph Paxton's connectional intelligence enabled the Crystal Palace to be built quickly and economically. It was very new for its time. But his creation was more than an example of connectional intelligence; it was a structure used for one of the first modern milestones of connectivity. The Crystal Palace housed the Great Exhibition of 1851, a celebration of culture and industry featuring over 100,000 exhibits by 15,000 participants. Some of the rare sights in the Crystal Palace included a printing press that could turn out 5,000 copies of the popular *Illustrated London News* in an hour, a giant fire engine from Canada and what was at the time the largest diamond in the world, the Koh-i-Noor diamond from India, which weighed in at an amazing 793 carats uncut.

Six million people visited the Crystal Palace, almost a third of the entire population of Great Britain at the time. People left the fair changed—with more knowledge, more understanding, more insight than they ever had before. They experienced the power, speed and magnitude of changes coming in their times—and this shared knowledge would affect their lives in ways large and small for decades to come.

We can and do look to the natural world to connect ideas and inspire solutions that we might not have reached otherwise. As H. G. Wells wrote in his genre-defining science fiction novel, *The Time Machine,* "Nature never appeals to intelligence until habit and instinct are useless. There is no intelligence where there is no need of change."[23] More recently, Ben Silbermann found the inspiration to build the collector's paradise that is Pinterest, not from collages or mood boards, but from his fascination with his childhood bug collection.

It's no secret that while technology has brought about amazing innovation, we continue to leave too heavy a footprint on the planet. Zimbabwe-born architect Mick Pearce wanted to create a beautiful, modern edifice that was at the same time energy-efficient. So he did as Joseph Paxton did: he turned to nature. In designing Eastgate Centre, a major shopping center and office complex in central Harare, Zimbabwe, Mick turned to termite mounds for inspiration.

Termites are ingenious creatures. They require a constant temperature of 86 to 88 degrees Fahrenheit. But temperatures in Zimbabwe are far from constant. Night temperatures can drop to 35 degrees Fahrenheit, but in the afternoon, the temperature can hit 104 Fahrenheit.[24] Termites regulate the heat in their homes by digging something called a breeze-catcher. They carve out chambers in the wet mud at the base to cool the air; hot air rises and is dispersed through a flue to the top. To keep the heat/humidity ratio constant, termites regularly open up new tunnels and close off others.

Though an architect by training, Mick had a passion for understanding natural ecosystems and realized these two fields—architecture and ecology—were interconnected. As Janine Benyus points out in *Biomimicry: Innovation Inspired by Nature,* plants, animals and microbes have done everything we want to do—without polluting the planet or becoming addicted to fossil fuel. So, she asks, "What better models could there be?"[25]

Mick designed a building with thick masonry walls and an interior atrium that couldn't be more post-modern: steel-lattice girders, suspended walkways, even bridges. But that's where the human design ended. Inspired by the termites, he installed fans that suck fresh air from the atrium and push it upwards through hollow spaces under the floors and into offices via baseboard vents. The air warms as it rises, then is expelled through forty-eight brick funnels. By day, big fans cool the building by moving air seven times an hour; at night, smaller fans move two changes of air an hour through the building. This ventilation system costs 10 percent of what a comparable air-conditioning unit would. The building uses 35 percent less energy than six conventional buildings in Harare combined.[26]

Mick Pearce's design saved the Eastgate owners $3.5 million in energy costs. His design also brought a great economic benefit to the developing business communities in East Africa—the tenants in Eastgate, because of the ingenious design, paid rents that were 20 percent lower than tenants in the surrounding buildings.[27]

His process relied on what we consider the three great questions of connectional intelligence. First, he asked, what is the problem? He needed to design a modern, environmentally friendly building in a city in Africa that did not have strong models of either. Then he asked, what if? What if nature, specifically termites, might provide the solution?

Mick asked the third question: does it matter? And the answer was a re-sounding yes. It mattered to the environment, it mattered to the developing economic infrastructure of Zimbabwe and—as it turned out—it mattered to many people in design communities all around the world. When Mick was awarded the Prince Claus Award for his Eastgate development, the jury committee wrote: "With this building, Mick Pearce has tossed the norms of architectural correctness out of the window and looked to nature and local cultures for a solution to sustainability."[28]

This goes to show that local culture and the realities of the natural geo-climatic region have much to teach those who are willing to reject standardized ready-made solutions. His building stands not only as a defense of diversity in the face of the homogenizing forces of globalized practice, but also as a defense against a backward-looking refusal to engage with the modern world. Mick Pearce has probably moved further away from the lip service the profession usually gives to enhancing sustainability and diversity than any architect in the world today. His great achievement has been to come up with a truly innovative and successful alternative to the all-glass high-rises that tropical countries tend to import from the North.

Like Mick Pearce, Chris Fischer is passionate about using connectional intelligence to do more than pay lip service to environmentalism and sustainability. For as long as he could remember, Chris was enamored of the ocean. "All of my life, ever since I was a kid, I had this passion for the water," he said.[29] He was twenty-nine when his brothers sold the family business, which left him (excuse the pun) at sea. His share of the earnings were not enough to retire on, but he did take a few months off to consider his options. Because he loved the sea, he decided to do his thinking on a sailboat, off the coast of California. Living on the ocean for months at a time was a revelation, and he realized that a great many Americans are completely disconnected from what's going on in our oceans and what it means to our collective future.

One of the things that Chris learned during this time of reassessment in his life was the importance of great white sharks. "Most people think sharks are invincible, but they are in real danger," he explained. "Sharks are the lions of the ocean. They're the great balance. If we lose our sharks, we lose our oceans."[30] Chris discovered that fishermen were killing 200,000 sharks a day, over 73 million a year—and sending most to China, where shark-fin soup remains a prized delicacy.[31]

As he got involved in research and exploring trips, primarily tagging sharks to create an open database for scientific study, Chris discovered a big disconnect between the practical knowledge of fishing captains capturing sharks, scientists in the academic world competing for grants and published papers, media journalists typecasting the great white sharks as a dangerous threat to humans and policy officials dealing with endangered species. "I realized that I was not going to be able to make a global impact for the future of the ocean if I was only a well-known fisherman," he said. "I needed to become the greatest ocean explorer of our time, the [Robinson] Crusoe of our time."[32] Humble he is not, but admittedly, it takes a lot of moxie to decide to take on a cause as big as the ocean and a lot of courage, maybe even bravado, to go nose to nose with the great white sharks.

"Most people think sharks are invincible, but they are in danger. Sharks are the lions of the ocean. They're the great balance. If we lose our sharks, we lose our ocean."

Chris created shows for the National Geographic Channel and the History Channel, receiving $20 million to be on the shows. This not only offered Ocearch global reach, but helped to fund it, as he donated half of his income. He hosted *Offshore Adventures* from 2002 to 2009. Audiences responded enthusiastically to his 180-episode chronicle of fishing, free-diving and conservation—it was America's "most watched outdoor television show."[33] He also impressed TV critics; *Offshore Adventures* won two Emmy Awards. The White House even reached out to Chris for advice on responsible fisheries management, and in 2007, President Bush joined Chris on a tour of the Chesapeake Bay.

But when the show ended, his mission was still unfulfilled. So he started inviting scientists, fisherman and the press—print, Internet and television—to join him on shark tagging expeditions. His vessel, the *MV Ocearch,* utilizes a custom 75,000-pound capacity hydraulic platform designed to safely lift mature sharks. This gives a multidisciplinary research team access to the sharks, enabling the team to conduct up to twelve studies in approximately fifteen minutes on a live mature shark. Only in this age of the rise of connectional intelligence could a young man from Louisville, Kentucky, without an advanced degree of any sort, travel out to the ocean, ask the powerful questions that would bring a major environmental problem to light and then create a platform on which the brightest minds from all around the world could gather to collaboratively work on solutions.

Experts, fishermen, and the press were quick to take Chris up on his invitation, and the ship soon filled with guests. Communication about the work was connected across every distribution platform—print, Internet, local TV, national TV and global TV. Chris remembers the insight that changed everything: "If we were totally inclusive and open-sourced everything, our scale exploded."[34]

He approached socially responsible companies like Caterpillar (the *MV Ocearch* uses Caterpillar engines and generators) who helped fund his mission. And he invited leading oceanic authorities such as Dr. Michael Dormeier of the Marine Conservation Science Institute. Dr. Dormeier's life's work has been acknowledged as the most comprehensive white shark study in the world. Chris's collaboration with academics has brought over fifty researchers from over twenty institutions to the *MV Ocearch* and has led to more than three dozen major research papers.

In 2013, Chris and the Ocearch team launched a comprehensive series of lesson plans for grades six through eight. With Ocearch's committed outreach to schools, Chris's legacy will include all the young people who will grow into adulthood knowledgeable about and connected to the ocean.

Ocearch also has become a resource to beach authorities. When one tagged shark was less than a mile from the coast of Florida beaches, Chris Fischer, working on his laptop in Utah, saw it. He alerted beach authorities of potential sharks in the area using the tracking tool, and no one was hurt. Today, ordinary citizens and beach safety professionals can use Ocearch's online platform to be on the lookout for sharks near their neighborhood beaches.

What Chris did, using his gifts of connectional intelligence, is discover a way to build widespread connection based on the strengths, needs, curiosity and convictions of a wide array of groups and individuals. By creating excitement around his topic, touching people's passion for the sea and creating and making open the best database on great white sharks, Chris gained an audience and community exponentially greater than the audience he reached on television. "We've gone from an audience of 25 million on TV to 120 million in press coverage," he said.[35] Shark Tracker, one of Ocearch's mapping tools, uses satellite technology to track the navigational pattern of tagged sharks. Anyone can use Shark Tracker, from kids to PhDs. Its impact goes beyond pure data. Indeed, the tool is contributing to the next generation of young people who are learning about sharks in their natural environment.

Success has brought major innovation, especially in the breadth of media Chris now reaches. Success has also brought Chris closer to his ultimate goal: public and private partnerships to save the ocean.

Chris has become a partner to Fortune 500 heavyweights like Landrys, Yamaha and Caterpillar. "What I'm working toward is to crowd-fund Fortune 500 companies to solve the major problems of our planet, like marine debris," he says. "I want to collaborate with business, media and academia to solve trillion-dollar problems. As they're saving the planet, they'll also be growing their businesses."[36]

He has a not-so-secret weapon: He's the hub of a collaborative network combining academics and fishermen that also touches millions of people who simply have passion for the sea. "What I think we're unleashing is the capacity to disrupt all of these old institutional approaches and put the public first," he says.[37] And there are no resources more powerful, he says, than an involved public, a fully leveraged set of Fortune 500 companies and engaged government.

It's hard to imagine that a shark guy would be the one to create a model of connection that brings together so many worlds and has impact on so many levels. But Chris Fischer has been fueled by not only a passion to get big things done but by the layman's gift of not having a preconceived notion of how to do the work of the challenges of his journey. He tried everything. He knocked on every open door and he invited in all interested parties. When we do this, we not only accomplish our most ambitious, audacious goals, we also connect with people we've never imagined, creating an environment in which connectional intelligence flourishes.

10

THE REALLY GOOD NEWS

THE TIME IS NOW. THERE IS SO MUCH TO BE DONE IN THE world, and every person needs to do their part. We hope that you now see, as we do, that you can access connectional intelligence, in all its variations, to pursue your dreams. It is not just for younger generations, with their natural predisposition for being connected, but a rising tide for all of us if we choose to embrace it. And we need each other, each with our unique capabilities, perspectives and experience, to get those big things done.

Connectional intelligence is both fun and rewarding. It will change your sense of belonging in the world, and help you discover your purpose. It can take you beyond your personal goals—allowing you to help others and change the world in ways even you didn't imagine. It can also lead you to people you might otherwise miss—who might enrich your lives forever.

We hope that traveling with us in this book has let you see that you can activate your connectional intelligence and help others do the same. We hope this book inspires you to do just that, and guides your journey.

Remember our promise at the beginning of the book:

Take a Dream.
Add Connection.
Dream Bigger.
Get Big Things Done.

Now it's your turn to realize this promise in your life. Everyone can benefit from connectional intelligence. Where will you go? How will you take this journey with others? It's a journey that starts with your dream, your passion, and your willingness to know yourself.

We have found chronicling connectional intelligence to be a radically hopeful exploration. As we continue to ride and study the wave of connectional intelligence, one of the things that most excites us is that this rising tide of connectional intelligence is not limited to those with access and privilege. Connectional intelligence isn't just about bold-faced names or ivory towers.

Co-author Saj-nicole says she found the story of Ron and his one-ton pumpkin moving "because today Ron's connectional intelligence can fly in a way that thirty years ago would not have been possible. He can connect, learn, create the first one-ton pumpkin—and in so doing, feed the world at a scale that he could not have imagined."

Co-author Erica says she is "deeply inspired and humbled that you do not have to be a 'super-genius' to have connectional intelligence. All you need to do is connect with your full heart, mind, and brain power."

We all know we are living in challenging times. Organizations, networks and communities are more interconnected than ever before. In our fast-changing world, the people and organizations who harness the power of connectional intelligence will be in a position to lead. The rest—those who stay disconnected, move slowly or not at all—may struggle, or even suffer. If you learn to activate the connectional intelligence within yourself and those around you, you can become unstoppable.

The message that we as authors wish to convey is: We all can do this. With our passion and our caring, we can learn, connect and create. And when our ideas combust, we can change lives we could not have imagined reaching. Not because we set out to do so, but because we expressed our connectional intelligence. We believe that when we join together we can solve our hardest problems and anything is possible.

One last thing: if you got anything out of this book, we're hoping you'll do something else for us. Give this copy to someone else. Ask them to read it. Urge them to activate their full connectional intelligence. Share your story with us. Spread the word.

We return to our question to you at the beginning of the book:

If you could multiply what you know in your head and your heart, your IQ and EQ, by the power of everyone you've ever e-mailed or could contact by social media and other technology, what would you do? *Which is, of course, to say, if you could do anything, what would you do? The choice is yours.*

PART 3

PULLING IT ALL TOGETHER

Your Get Big Things Done Handbook

CONNECTIONAL INTELLIGENCE IS MUCH BIGGER AND MORE powerful than networking. In the late 1990s and 2000s, the research on networks took off. In 2002, Duke University professor Nan Lin wrote the groundbreaking book *Social Capital,* which argued for the importance of using social connections and social relations in achieving goals. He theorized that "it is who you know" as well as "what you know," that makes a difference in life and society. At the time, it was a pioneering point of view, and the book title has since become common shorthand for the web of connections that vaults some people ahead of others who have seemingly similar talent and drive.

More than a decade later, this thinking seems narrow and limited and is in need of an update. Connectional intelligence—the ability to combine the world's diversity of people, networks, disciplines and resources, forging connections that create value, meaning and breakthrough results—means not only that power and influence are more graspable than ever, but that we can now achieve more than we ever imagined in *conjunction* with others.

At the beginning of the book, we shared with you our simple manifesto:

Take a Dream.
Add Connection.
Dream Bigger.
Get Big Things Done.

Now we're going to dive deeper, and focus on how you can use what we've presented in this book to make practical and powerful changes in your life and work. Since there are as many ways to be connectionally intelligent as there are people, we're offering up several different ways to work with this material:

- **5 C's of Connectional Intelligence:** A guide to use alone or with a team to understand the most common attributes of connectionally intelligent people.
- **CxQ Role Models:** A guide that offers up a set of role models to help you think about moving in the world in connectionally intelligent ways, from the *Seeker* to the *Activist,* from the *Dreamer* to the *Empathetic Entrepreneur.* If you learn best by examples and stories, this section is for you.
- **Connectional Intelligence Quiz:** A mini-assessment you can use to gauge how well you are using your connectional intelligence, the 5 C's, and examine which CxQ role models you might want to partner with, based on your strengths and weaknesses, to get big things done.
- *Get Big Things Done* **Work Plan:** Five big questions to ask yourself when you are trying to get big things done. To develop the most thoughtful and revealing responses, the questions are open-ended—questions you can continue to ask yourself over time.
- *Get Big Things Done* **Manager Guide:** A short guide that provides a structure for managers to effectively apply this

material with their own teams. This guide helps identify a
team's overall strengths and weaknesses across the 5 C's, and
also shows how to leverage CxQ role models to get big things
done.

- *Get Big Things Done* **Really Good News:** Here are some
  powerful reminders of the power of connectional intelligence
  in your life and work. Turn to this section when you need to
  reflect, re-orient and recharge.

- *Get Big Things Done* **Reading Discussion Guide:** Now
  that you've read this book, we want you to keep thinking and
  talking. Use this group discussion guide to go out and debate
  these ideas with your community, in your book club, on your
  blog or on a social networking site.

- *Get Big Things Done* **Recap:** This book has covered a lot
  of ground—and you might not be able to instantly recall
  everything in it. So here you'll find:
  - The definition of connectional intelligence
  - GBTD Twitter summary
  - GBTD coffee shop talking points
  - GBTD refresher course.

5 C'S OF CONNECTIONAL INTELLIGENCE

In our research, we've identified five attributes that occur again and again in the stories of connectionally intelligent people. To bring out your CxQ and get big things done, you should first understand the 5 C's of connectional intelligence.

- *Curiosity,* or the ability to frame and ask questions from different contexts to gain new perspectives.
- *Combination,* or the ability to take different ideas, resources or products and combine them to create new concepts, new ways of thinking and get surprising results.
- *Community,* or the ability to bring people together to create, spark new ideas and develop care and understanding.
- *Courage,* the ability to venture, persevere and withstand uncertainty, fear or even danger when connecting ideas or initiating difficult conversations, as well as the courage to keep these ideas and connections alive and amplify them where necessary.
- *Combustion,* or the ability to mobilize and curate diverse networks to act in pursuit of a goal.

Let's examine the 5 C's in the context of some of the CxQ stories we've already looked at:

THE BIG PUMPKIN

First, let's revisit Ron Wallace. Remember him? Ron was the guy from the smallest state in the United States whose lifelong ambition was to win a spot in the *Guinness World Records*. Ron, if it's not clear by now, was **curious**. He wanted to find out everything he could about every industry and fact related to his passion, including potato farming, soil science and how funguses work. First he learned all he could about growing pumpkins, followed by fruit and vegetable growing, and then he began collating data from everywhere he could think of. This took **courage:** to go more widely; to keep doing what others told him couldn't be done; to make contact with leading scientists; and to persist until he got what he wanted.

When Ron joined a statewide pumpkin growers' association and became an active member of BigPumpkins.com, he evolved to find value and **community** between two distinct groups—the pumpkin community and the scientific community. At some point, Ron decided to **combine** everything he knew—soil science research, potato farming research, strategies about when and how to time his crop. When The Freak II broke the world record, Ron Wallace's story **combusted**, en route to accessing a larger audience. Today, Ron gives talks across the world, scientists who once considered him an irritant court him for his experience, and he's been able to use his platform to launch a courageous conversation about the dangers of commercial fertilizer.

CRISIS TEXT LINE

Let's revisit Nancy Lublin from DoSomething.org. Nancy was always a genius **community** builder and **combuster**—she built DoSomething.org to mobilize over two million teens across the US to engage in the social issues that mattered most to them. When disturbing and alarming texts began to appear on the text platform, she used her **curiosity** to ask a new set of questions: How can we help? Who can we connect to who can help these teens? She was **courageous** enough to **combine** her resources with new **communities**—social workers, teen health experts, health clinics—and create Crisis Text Line, a texting hotline for teens in crisis. But she didn't stop there. She also asked which other **communities** could benefit from the data coming from Crisis Text Line and is now **combusting** the Crisis Text Line data to create a real-time database on teens and their troubles. She uses this data to reach new **communities**—public policy officials, school administrators and educators—to shape public policy related to teenagers and their needs. Nancy reminds us that sometimes connectional intelligence is something that you use to get big things done, and sometimes CxQ is a matter of being open to act in the shifting landscape.

TERMITES

The ventilation system at the Eastgate Centre in Harare, Zimbabwe requires only 10 percent of the energy use of buildings with traditional ventilation systems. For this you can credit architect Mick Pearce, who had the idea of applying lessons learned from looking at termite mounds to shopping mall designs. Mick, a Zimbabwean, had a profound commitment to the African **community** and expressed this in his determination to build beautiful, modern and sustainable buildings that also reflected the truth of local cultures. He **combined** this commitment with his insatiable **curiosity**, which led him to discover that termites keep temperatures steady inside their homes by carefully opening and carefully closing their mounds' heating and cooling vents, a fact he applied to his design. He created a system in which hot air soaks into the base of the building and is then propelled upwards toward a series of chimneys. Mick led a **courageous** conversation by tossing conventional tenets of modern architecture out of the window and looking to nature and local cultures for a solution to sustainability. Mick **combined** this "termite technology" to the Eastgate Centre he was tasked to build. Today, his work has **combusted**, leading to the creation of the Zimbabwe-based TERMES project, which uses digital technology to scan termite mounds in order to map their architecture in painstaking detail. Its mission is to help provide the world with a template for creating self-regulating buildings and even cities.

USHAHIDI IN HAITI

Responding to reports that over 100,000 Haitians were probably dead, and fearing for close friends working in Port-au-Prince he hadn't heard from, Patrick Meier, a doctoral research fellow at Tufts University's Fletcher School, **courageously** launched a live crisis map of Haiti from his office outside Boston—and then just kept on mapping.

Half of Haiti had power; the other half didn't. Patrick began **combining** tweets, YouTube videos and other social media postings and updates. He brought in a **community** of colleagues to help him track every piece of incoming data and called on student volunteers to work online. He also **combined** with Boston members of the Haitian diaspora. Working from a computer lab on the Tufts campus, together they translated tweets and status updates from Haitian-Creole into English. When relief organizations, the US military and the Haitian government recognized what was happening, Ushahidi **combusted**. Within days, the US military was using Ushahidi to help locate missing people and redirect survivors to safer ground.

CXQ ROLE MODELS

There are three categories of connectionally intelligent people—*Thinkers, Enablers* and *Connection Executors. Thinkers* help spark and generate the big ideas, *Enablers* create the structures and forces to get big things done and *Connection Executors* mobilize all the people and resources needed to get big things done.

In our research, we've identified that these three categories of connectionally intelligent people have varying strengths among the 5 C's. *Thinkers* have high levels of curiosity, combination and courage. *Enablers* have high levels of community, combination and courage. *Connection Executors* have high levels of combustion, community and courage.

To help you think about where you fit amongst the three categories, we will discuss ten CxQ role models in this section by looking at the people you've met in this book.

TABLE 1

Thinkers	Enablers	Connection Executors
Dreamers	Inspired Leaders	Mix Masters
Adventurers	Advocates	Activists
Seekers	Creative Company Individuals	Empathetic Entrepreneurs
		Disruptors

Most of us play many different roles in our lives, often simultaneously. So while you may be a *Dreamer* in your private life, launching a business on Etsy or pitching a new invention to a platform like Quirky, you're a *Mix Master* at work, bringing together disparate groups toward a common, innovative goal. With your family, you may be an *Advocate,* fundraising for a cause you believe in that affects someone you love dearly, while playing the *Disruptor* at work, creating a game-changing platform like Airbnb. When you decide to go back to school, that's the *Seeker* itching to hit the books.

While you may relate to some of these CxQ roles in greater and lesser ways, we encourage you to peruse the CxQ role models that speak to you. If you look at your own stories, patterns, fears and talents, what would you say is "typical" of you? How do other people describe you? (And if you're up for it, ask your friends for help with this. Their answers may surprise you.)

We also encourage you to look for CxQ role models closer to home. Identifying someone's role will allow you to interact with them on the most effective level. Is your boss a number-crunching *Seeker* or more of an *Inspired Leader?* Is your child a *Mix Master* or an *Adventurer?* How many of your friends are *Empathetic Entrepreneurs* and how many are *Activists?* What about those next-door neighbors nagging you to compost—are they devoted *Advocates?*

Observe the CxQ role models operating in the people you encounter, whether at home or in the workplace. And what about the way people present themselves on Facebook, Twitter and other digital platforms? What CxQ role models might they be communicating, intentionally or without even realizing it? As you become more adept at identifying the CxQ role models in those around you, you will become more comfortable with spotting your own CxQ role in action.

Because we know that these ten roles just begin to hint at the universe of connectionally intelligent people and how they operate, where and how they win big and what they have to teach us all, we'll be adding more roles to the digital world of this book and on our website and through social media. Remember, no one is a complete expert at connectional intelligence, so we're showing many different examples of people from our book who are taking actions to increase their connectional intelligence. We'll also be inviting you to share stories of individuals that you believe demonstrate exceptional connectional intelligence.

THE THINKERS

These are the people who generate the groundbreaking ideas. They help see the big picture and imagine all possibilities.

5 C's Strengths: Curiosity, Combination, Courage
CxQ Role Models: Dreamers, Adventurers, Seekers

THE DREAMERS

Traits: creative, idealistic, patient: a visionary with strength of imagination

Description: Dreamers are the heart center of the connectional intelligence universe. They are the people who have the patience, the courage, the vision and the strength to imagine the impossible and get big things done. We can see these traits in Ron Wallace's quest to grow a 2,000-pound pumpkin, in John Green's community of Nerdfighters and in Shiza Shahid's and Malala Yousafzai's audacious, breathtaking goal to aid and harness the underutilized brain power of 600 million girls in the developing world who face long-held institutional and political barriers to their education. *Dreamers* are almost always engaging with the future, imagining the possibilities and what might be next. They are most comfortable among imaginative people with inventive ideas and an original take on life. And they are always asking, "What if?"

Examples: Ron Wallace (Chapter 3), Shiza Shahid and Malala Yousafzai (Chapter 5), John Green and Nerdfighters (Chapter 8)

Tools:
  1. **Share your ideas with different communities and networks.**
     Sharing comes easy for a *Dreamer*. You're naturally drawn to

stimulating conversation, particularly with people who think differently than you do. Keep putting yourself in places where you can see life through their eyes. Spend time with new people who encourage you to see things from new perspectives and other angles. When Ron Wallace dreamed of growing a big pumpkin, he tested his ideas with leading scientists and pumpkin associations. When Shiza Shahid saw the opportunity to leverage all the energy around Malala, she quickly began to build resources beyond her traditional community—to engage innovators, doers, governments, local leaders, nonprofits and large institutions. And when John Green started creating YouTube Nerdfighter videos, he bridged a community of gays, transgender kids, teens with diseases, victims of bullies and just plain smart and sensitive teens—more than a million members.

2. **Build alliances with partners who have common interests and missions, but different skills, to support your goal.** *Dreamers* require partners to turn their ideas into action. Ron Wallace worked with leading scientists who could help him test new soil samples. *Dreamers* need to partner with CxQ role models like the *Activist, Advocate* or *Seeker* to take the next step in getting big things done. When you surround yourself with others who challenge you, you can find wisdom in the exchange of ideas, and fight your way to breakthroughs. When *Dreamers* like Ron, Shiza and John bring diverse groups with shared passions together, that's when the magic happens.

3. **Leverage what's been done before.** Find commonalities with your big dreams and what already exists. Be open to the various ways people are already taking action around your dream and learn to work with them in new ways. We saw this both in the Malala Fund's partnership with the UN and women's groups around the world and the movement Ron Wallace created teaching people how to grow bigger, healthier vegetables and

his methods ultimately influencing farming in places like India. We saw this as well when John Green built partnerships with like-minded communities such as Kiva, World Vision and Save the Children, which ultimately helped his Nerdfighters increase their social impact.

Words to Live By:

"Without leaps of imagination or dreaming, we lose the excitement of possibilities. Dreaming, after all is a form of planning."[1]

—Gloria Steinem

THE ADVENTURERS

Traits: independent, unconventional, courageous: a trailblazer

Description: Adventurers are people who dare to go out into the world to seek new experiences, unchartered territory and novel undertakings. They go out and discover problems: when they employ connectional intelligence, they get big things done far and wide. *Adventurers* reject labels, boxes or constraints of any kind, and accept risk as part of the adventure. We saw an example of this in Dusty Payne, the young surfer who studied the techniques of athletes in adjacent sports—skateboarders, windsurfers, mountain bikers and motocross champions around the world—to help him invent the "Superman" move. Chris Fischer, the ocean explorer, is another prime example of an *Adventurer.* He turned his passion for great white sharks into a collaborative, inclusive and open-source network that enabled local scientists, academics and citizens to attain previously unattainable data on great white sharks and other endangered species.

Examples: Luis von Ahn from Duolingo (Chapter 7), Chris Fischer and Ocearch (Chapter 9), Dusty Payne and the surfers (Chapter 3)

Tools:

1. **Leverage your mastered skills to get out of the box.** Start with what you know well and think about how you can use it to build and test new ideas. Luis von Ahn was a leading expert in dual-purpose technology and combining human brainpower and computers to solve large scale problems, skills he used when he developed Duolingo. Chris Fischer became a media guru, then used his TV shows and media coverage to turn his media savvy into a movement for open-source research, sharing data in near real-time for free on the Shark Tracker, and enabling students and the public to learn alongside PhDs.

2. **Engage regularly with a supportive hub or community in which you can test your ideas and turn them into action.** Chris Fischer has a tight, connected team at Ocearch, made up of scientists, fishermen and media. Luis von Ahn leveraged his lab at Carnegie Mellon University to take his adventurous ideas and turn them into practical applications like reCAPTCHA and Duolingo.

3. **Study adjacencies—activities and topics loosely connected to your primary interest—to identify new ways of addressing challenges.** Dusty Payne and his surfer teammates analyzed footage of extreme sports from windsurfing to motorcycling, leading to the creation of the "Superman," the move with which he won the surfing championship. Chris Fischer spent countless days and nights exploring the ocean with fisherman and scientists, leading him to create Ocearch.

Words to Live By:

"One doesn't discover new lands without consenting to lose site of the shore . . ."[2]

—Andre Gide

THE SEEKERS

Traits: curious, autonomous, bold: a provocateur

Description: Seekers are people who ask the big, beautiful questions that move thoughts to action. They pursue knowledge for the sake of knowledge and find truth in all its expressions. *Seekers* learn for the sheer love of learning. They look closely and consider all the options before acting and cultivate wisdom to improve life for themselves and others.

In a world of ubiquitous connection, *Seekers* thrive; they are surfing the web, doing scientific research, shopping online, writing a blog post or firing off e-mails. *Seekers* look for knowledge and understanding of the full spectrum of what can be grasped by the human mind. We've seen seekers across all walks of life in our stories, like graduate student Thomas Herndon, CrowdMed founder Jared Heyman and inventor Ed Melcarek.

Examples: Thomas Herndon (Chapter 3), Jared Heyman and Crowd-Med (Chapter 9), Ed Melcarek (Chapter 3)

Tools:

1.   **Keep asking the question "what if the accepted wisdom/ same old assumptions are not true?"** *Seekers* notice something different happening and turn it into a question, taking it in a new direction. When Thomas Herndon discovered the error in an accepted economics model, he asked: What if the leading economists are wrong? What if someone knew? How can I find the answer? If you are a *Seeker,* you might be asking similar questions and fueling your passion for exploring why things are the way they are.

2.   **Look at what you already know.** Ask yourself: What do I already know that connects me to something different from

what I know? Jared Heyman ran a survey company which gave him the knowledge that led to founding CrowdMed. Through his insatiable curiosity, Ed Melcarek quickly solved a major Colgate challenge by bringing what he already knew as a physicist to what had been labeled a chemistry problem. Thomas Herndon realized that while just a student, he had the opportunity to take the reins to fix a major error in economic theory that was affecting global organizations like the World Bank and the UN.

3. **Engage in forums and smaller groups that allow you to ask better questions.** For inventors like Ed Melcarek, a "forum" may look more like Quirky or InnoCentive. For the digital *Seeker,* a "smaller group" could be an update on a Facebook group, a Twitter discussion based on a hashtag, in Quora forums, or on Pinterest boards. Use smaller groups to build support structures to help you to keep asking the courageous questions, just like Thomas Herndon did by gaining support from his professors.

Words to Live By:

> *"Truth is rarely pure and never simple."*[3]

> —Oscar Wilde

THE ENABLERS

These are the people who create the structures, forces and teams used to get big things done.

   5 C's Strengths: Community, Combination, Courage
   CxQ Role Models: Inspired Leaders, Advocates, Creative
      Company Individuals

THE INSPIRED LEADERS

Traits: purposeful, team-focused, driven: an initiator of positive change

Description: Inspired Leaders ask the right questions. They help employees and colleagues build an architecture to achieve ambitious goals and use their influence to make a difference in people's lives. They take risks and assume responsibility for the group's risks. They also empower and enable *Creative Company Individuals* on the team and are deeply comfortable with change. They take charge of situations for the sake of achieving maximum results. We've seen examples of inspired leaders in Ben Kaufman, who brought product development to a wider community through Quirky, and Pat Mitchell, who became a passionate mentor and leader for women around the world, thanks to the TEDx-Women movement she built.

Examples: Ben Kaufman from Quirky (Chapter 4), the Colgate executive team (Chapter 4), Pat Mitchell (Chapter 6)

Tools:

   1. **Break or reverse "stupid rules" or processes that are holding
      back progress.** For example, Ben Kaufman, CEO of Quirky,

asked: Why does it take a kitchenware company two years and
seven months to design and manufacture a potato peeler? Aware
that issues around financing, engineering and distribution
stand in most people's way of converting a great idea into a
product that can be brought to market, Kaufman's company,
Quirky, breaks the traditional rules. Kaufman asks consumers
to submit their idea for an invention, a global community
votes in a winner and—twice a month—Quirky designs and
manufactures two products, everything from hip iPhone cases to
electronics to kitchen gadgets to housewares. The company has
transformed how the world thinks about product development.

2. **Ask new crowds and communities to help.** Encourage
collaboration between communities in a way in which everyone
has a voice at the table: community voting, anonymous input
and gaming platforms like Quirky, CrowdMed and *Foldit*.
Can you partner up *Creative Company Individuals* inside
organizations or *Seekers* outside your organizations? For
example, when the Colgate executive team reached out to a
group of solvers, people they normally wouldn't have contacted
due to the constraints of the traditional hiring process, they
instantly found outside physicist Ed Melcarek, who solved their
packaging problem. When Pat Mitchell launched TEDWomen,
she also invited communities from college campuses, corporate
offices and small-town neighborhoods to host their own local
TEDxWomen events, leading to gatherings in far-off locales
such as Mongolia and Saudi Arabia.

3. **Fail forward and fail fast.** Projects that encounter roadblocks
or end in failure have great value, but only if you can identify
the reasons and then learn the lessons. There are always internal
factors and external conditions that will help you shape your
next move.

Words to Live By:

"You have everything you need to build something far bigger than yourself."[4]

—Seth Godin

THE ADVOCATES

Traits: caring, supportive, empathetic: a good listener with a desire to give back

Description: Advocates are motivated to act on behalf of others. They help people achieve their hopes and dreams within the fabric of their communities. *Advocates* have a fire that is automatically ignited when they see a way to make a difference and identify how they can bring about change. They give their all so that the lives of others will improve.

Think about Karen Brocklebank (Noah's mom), Jeannie Peeper, or Allana Maiden. In each case, their mission was more than a nice idea; it drove them to make a difference in a major way. An *Advocate*'s involvement doesn't have to happen on a grand scale. It could be answering phones at a crisis center or guiding visitors around a community garden. Their GBTD mission may not seem to have the same scope or gravitas as other stories, but the clarity of why it matters and what they want to do is critical for *Advocates*.

Examples: Jeannie Peeper (Chapter 9), Karen Brocklebank (Chapter 6), Allana Maiden (Chapter 6)

Tools:

1. **Pick a cause that matters to you and focus on why it matters to the people you want to serve.** If you don't already have an issue you are invested in, pick something that will energize you. With the Internet, it's never been easier to find a cause

to commit to. While you're looking, listen to your gut. What issue would you like to see resolved? Is there an area that moves you—health, women's issues or animal rights? Is there a location you're drawn to—Darfur, perhaps, or India or Appalachia? What skills do you have that you can apply toward solving a problem? You may not be a doctor or public health expert, but perhaps you have a media or accounting background, are tech savvy, or have a way with people or words. Once you are clear on what cause you want to address, go out and figure out why it matters for the people you want to serve. Allana Maiden quickly realized that the creation of a survivor bra for her mother presented an opportunity to help many—there were thousands of petition signers who had a common mission and were just as passionate as she was about her idea.

2. **Strategically target the communities and networks you want to reach and what you want from them.** Use the right tools to activate your networks. Noah's mom, Karen, used a Letters to Noah campaign to build a community. Allana Maiden set up a Change.org petition and asked for signatures. And Jeannie Peeper shared medical information with other FOP patients through e-mail newsletters. Also, look for points to bring the hubs together. For example, Jeannie Peeper leveraged her "FOP Connection" newsletter to pool resources to fund FOP research at the University of Pennsylvania.

3. **Define your metrics for success.** As an advocate, be sure to have your own version of success. Allana Maiden's metric for success was to become a strong advocate for her mother. Jeannie Peeper helped to shape the lives of future generations facing FOP. She inspired people to realize that it doesn't cost much to make a big difference—a simple bowl-a-thon or barbeque fundraiser can be an important step toward a lifetime of

improvements for people suffering with FOP and other rare diseases.

Words to Live By:

"A small body of determined spirits fired by an unquenchable faith in their mission can alter the course of history."[5]

—Mahatma Gandhi

THE CREATIVE COMPANY INDIVIDUALS

Traits: confident, courageous, entrepreneurial: an executor of ideas

Description: These men and women aren't (necessarily) coveting their boss's job or dreaming about breaking off to do their own thing. What they want is the freedom to get big things done within the structure of the companies they work for. They are the entrepreneurs working inside large organizations. When they find a good idea, *Creative Company Individuals* know how to turn it into a full action plan. When they use the power of their creative vision, they not only contribute to society, they also take risks that could potentially impact the future of their employees, their organization and their industry.

These men and women consistently connect with people who stimulate their out-of-the-box thinking. They reject the same old things and rarely think the same old thoughts. We see this in leaders like Bonin Bough from Mondelez, who organized his team to be prepared and relevant when it mattered most through the Oreo Super Bowl tweet, and Christie Smith, who translated "covering," a civil rights and policy concept, into a corporate diversity conversation, helping to transform the culture at Deloitte to one of inclusion. Additionally, Simon Willison from *The Guardian* enlisted more than 20,000 readers to shovel through over 170,000 MP expense reports in just a few days through a game-like interface that united all of the reader–reviewers in the goal of hitting the big "score."

Examples: Bonin Bough and the Oreo tweet (Chapter 4), Christie Smith (Chapter 8), Simon Willison and *The Guardian* (Chapter 7)

Tools:

1. **Gain trust and enlist a committed supervisor and/ or mentor.** In order to build trust and develop this type of relationship, start with daily tasks to show you are committed to long-term goals. For example, Bonin Bough had consistently built trust with headquarters by successfully taking smaller risks, before the big plunge. His team started by creating relevant real-time Oreo ads in Times Square a year before the Super Bowl tweet, which prepared them to be fast and relevant for Super Bowl XLVII.

2. **Create space and regular opportunities to practice innovation in ways that don't heavily affect the company's bottom line and/or threaten its position**. As a *Creative Company Individual* you can assess the company's culture and limits and work in a manner that helps the organization take a risk, but in a way that the company is willing to try. Engage groups with whom you have a natural affinity (cultures, hobbies, passions, generations) inside and outside your organization and identify how you can leverage these groups to solve problems across existing silos. The result may be radical change, but the approach will feel organic. At the same time, don't become burdened with consensus. Make sure to incorporate broad ideas and team members while preserving the core mission.

3. **Gain access to groundbreaking innovation inside and outside your field.** This could be everything from watching

TEDx events at your desk to negotiating for an expense budget
that allows you to attend three conferences a year. For example,
Christie Smith consistently found ways to learn new concepts,
which led to her application of the idea of "covering" to enhance
diversity and inclusion at Deloitte. She intentionally spent time
meeting with external experts on a monthly basis and attended
conferences with innovators outside her industry. When Simon
Willison at *The Guardian* built a "game-like" interface to reveal
MPs' expenses, the project was built on Django, an open-source
web framework that Simon and other developers had created
four years earlier. Django required three years of open-source
development and was one of the key reasons *The Guardian* was
able to act with speed when the British MPs' expenses were
released.

Words to Live By:

*"A rock pile ceases to be a rock pile the moment a single man contemplates
it, bearing within him the image of a cathedral."*[6]

—Antoine de Saint-Exupéry

THE CONNECTION EXECUTORS

These are the individuals who mobilize all the people, ideas and resources needed to get big things done.

5 C's Strengths: Combustion, Community, Courage

CxQ Role Models: Mix Masters, Activists, Empathetic
  Entrepreneurs, Disruptors

THE MIX MASTERS

Traits: open-minded, creative, synergistic: a cross-pollinator of ideas

Description: Mix Masters thrive when they reach out and connect intelligently beyond their particular fields. Drawing upon varied skills, *Mix Masters* are able to spot patterns, make connections and help facilitate multiple opportunities and intersection points. They take existing pieces of knowledge, ideas and memories and coalesce them into new concepts, products, ideas or arguments. They often approach life like scientists, testing hypotheses and reaching reasoned conclusions. We saw this in Hunter Hoffman who connected to other PhDs, gaming applications and therapy methods, which led him to understand how to use gaming as a distraction to help burn victims manage pain. Also, MIT Little Devices was filled with *Mix Masters* who devised a cooler called "CoolComply," which can run on electric power or solar cells, saving daily ice deliveries that cost $600 per year.

Examples: Hunter Hoffman (Chapter 6), Sugata Mitra (Chapter 6), José Gómez Márquez and the MIT Little Devices Lab (Chapter 4)

Tools:

1. **Observe the types of people and ideas that you let into your life.** You can pick your teachers, your friends, the books you read, the music you listen to and the movies you watch. You are a mashup of what you let into your life; you can see differently by connecting with new types of people, ideas and knowledge. Hunter Hoffman spent his days connecting with PhDs across disciplines, leading to his integration of gaming and burn therapy.

2. **Hold an hour of exploration time or "play" each week.** As a *Mix Master,* you need time to conceive and combine ideas, and to engage long enough to follow through. Sometimes this time is spent growing new skills (e.g., blogging, singing, playing a sport, programming). Sometimes this time is spent connecting to people from different disciplines or backgrounds. Notice how you apply connectional intelligence in what you are learning. At MIT Little Devices Lab, José Gómez Márquez and his team consistently spent time exploring DIY ideas by traveling to places like Honduras and India; they followed up these travels with "dedicated" time back at the lab where they incorporated the ideas they had discovered into DIY health technologies that could solve pressing needs in many communities.

3. **Use different types of connection tools to test your ideas.** When mixing new ideas, try using different tools to connect with new communities and networks (video, audio, gaming, Twitter, Facebook, Vine, Pinterest). Use these tools to bring communities together. For example, the Granny Cloud uses Skype videos to connect grandmothers with Indian children, thus helping grandmothers to make meaning in their own lives and play a critical role in the lives of young people.

Words to Live By:

> *"Nothing is entirely original—everything builds on what came before.*
> *Creativity is a combinatorial process—we create by taking existing pieces*
> *of knowledge, ideas, influences, memories, and experiences collected in the*
> *course of being alive and awake to the world, and fusing those together into*
> *new combinations that we call our own 'original' ideas."[7]*

—Maria Popova

THE ACTIVISTS

Traits: courageous, committed, organized: a change agent

Description: Activists are committed to righting wrongs; they are justice-oriented. When they employ connectional intelligence, *Activists* get really big things done, solving problems, saving lives and changing the world. *Activists* are good at forging alliances and connecting disparate groups. We saw an example of this in the story of Patrick Meier, who first learned of Ushahidi while in Kenya and jumped at the opportunity to use the mapping tool when the Haiti earthquake hit. And *Activist* Martha Payne, the nine-year-old school girl who called foul on her school district's pitifully unhealthy and criminally expensive school lunches, is a prime example of how someone can begin with an issue that is personal and then go global. Martha diverted donations generated by her blog to a charity called Mary's Meals, helping to build a new kitchen and fund healthy meals at a primary school in Malawi.

Examples: Patrick Meier and Ory Okolloh from Ushahidi (Chapter 5), Martha Payne (Chapter 6), Ahmed Abulhassan from Tahrir Supplies (Chapter 5) and Rainer Nõlvak from the Let's Do It campaign (Chapter 7)

Tools:

1. **Cultivate your networks, striving for as much diversity as possible, before you really need them.** Identify ties that help you engage and connect to new crowds and organizations. Forge relationships with people who are different from you in age, view, political perspective, educational background, career role and geographic location. For example, it was Patrick Meier's prior connection to Ushahidi in Kenya that led him to launch the Haiti Ushahidi effort while at graduate school in Cambridge, MA. You never know when prior knowledge could turn into a tool for saving lives half way across the world.

2. **Create spaces for new constituencies to join forces with you.** Reach beyond the usual suspects. Ahmed Abulhassan from Tahrir Supplies begged Egyptian celebrities via Twitter to support and re-tweet @TahrirSupplies, quickly gaining over 10,000 followers in days. Patrick Meier partnered with a new network—the Haitian diaspora—when he realized translating Haitian Creole into English was among the most pressing need during his Haiti Ushahidi efforts.

3. **Find ways to give back once you've broadened your networks and built your movement.** It's important to envision sweeping change, but when it comes to getting something accomplished, start small and give back to your local networks. Starting with a familiar issue can help. By mobilizing thousands of people through the NeverSeconds platform around a local issue, over time Martha was able to connect globally and donate $100,000 to Mary's Meals in Malawi. Through Let's Do It cleanup campaigns in over 110 countries, Rainer Nõlvak and his co-founders have created an "open virtual world waste map" and are launching a social network for mappers to find each other, see what their friends have mapped and update their data.

Words to Live By:

> *"What counts in life is not the mere fact that we have lived. It is what difference we have made to the lives of others that will determine the significance of the life we lead."*[8]

—Nelson Mandela

THE EMPATHETIC ENTREPRENEUR

Traits: passionate, tenacious, adaptable: a creative visionary

Description: This person wants to be his own boss, but also wants to fill a real need. *Empathetic Entrepreneurs* are creative and driven; they are authentic salespeople, not hustlers. They are those who stop and listen, enabling them to connect with their customers and fans on an emotional level, putting themselves in service to others. They collect data before they make a big move, building the fuel needed to push past challenges that arise and bring something creative and new to the world. Most importantly, they really listen, all along the way, making sure that the work they are doing is delivering something that people actually want. We've seen this in entrepreneurs like burqini creator Aheda Zanetti, lifestyle blogger and YouTube celebrity Michelle Phan and rapper-turned-change-agent Pharrell.

Examples: Aheda Zanetti (Chapter 8), Michelle Phan (Chapter 3), Pharrell (Chapter 8)

Tools:

1. **Broaden the possibilities of who you might serve.** If you spend time talking to people and observing their needs, creative ideas start to appear, but often they can help more constituencies than you might imagine. For example, Aheda Zanetti's move to Australia led her to create the world's first two-piece burqini, made

of lycra and with a hijab-style head covering, which allows Muslim women to be active on the beach and now serves non-Muslim women who want to be fully covered for many different reasons. Michelle Phan listens closely to her fans and has cultivated viewers from all around the world by discussing different styles from different cultures—from Korean celebrities to French teenagers.

2. **Fail fast and fail forward.** If you are an *Empathetic Entrepreneur,* you must dabble, play, mess around and experiment. It hardly matters if you are good at it or not at first. You can move on to another form or genre without having to worry about humiliation of failure. For example, Pharrell took a big risk when he moved away from the typical music persona of most famous rappers. He tied everything he was working on back to the sustaining purpose of being proud and genuine in his nerdiness (as opposed to the cool music industry persona he sometimes adopted) and the desire to make a difference in the lives of young people who were outsiders, like himself. This internal compass led to the greatest breakthrough of this career.

3. **Set up a system of incremental rewards to sustain your business over the long term.** Being an *Empathetic Entrepreneur* takes guts and requires structures that fuel your passion and energy. For example, the daily support and input Michelle Phan receives from her fans helps her to connect more deeply with her community and create new videos based on what her fans are asking for, and fuels her for her work. Take the time to build structures to re-energize and keep connecting with the deepest needs of who you serve.

Words to Live By:

"Believe in your idea, trust your instincts, and don't be afraid to fail."[9]

—Sara Blakely

THE DISRUPTORS

Traits: audacious, forward-thinking, fearless: a risk-taking leader

Description: *Disruptors* are groundbreaking pioneers who upend traditional wisdom and find new ways of solving problems. *Disruptors* live in a world of "yes, and" as opposed to "no, but." They don't play by society's rules; in fact, they often feel that rules are made to be broken. *Disruptors* have a fearless willingness to plunge into the unknown. They are first to market or first to take action for anything that is new. Innovators like Apple's Steve Jobs and Facebook's Mark Zuckerberg perfectly embody the *Disruptor* model, creating whole new worlds in the most cutting-edge fields—technology and the Internet. *Disruptors* do things in nontraditional ways and introduce radically new ideas into the culture. They gravitate toward people with active minds and stimulating conversation. We saw many disruptive leaders in this book: Salman Khan, who is changing how students learn in an "inverted classroom"; Gamal Sadek, the CEO of Bey2ollak who is transforming the traditional idea that if you can't fix the roads, you can't fix the traffic; and David Baker, who created a game to run protein folding combinations. *Disruptors* know that when we are all connected, we can ask questions that we couldn't have asked before.

Examples: Salman Khan (Chapter 3), Gamal Sadek (Chapter 7), David Baker (Chapter 7)

Tools:

1. **Notice patterns that upend current wisdom and then break or reverse "stupid rules" or processes.** Gamal Sadek reversed the belief that radio is the only way to track traffic and address transportation issues by launching Bey2ollak, using the #cairotraffic hashtag to source information. His mobile

application is now revolutionizing how citizens in Cairo tackle traffic issues and fix road infrastructure.

2. **Create a separate, informal space that is exclusively devoted to creative thinking and brainstorming.** Schedule a regular time for you and your colleagues to brainstorm new ideas, discuss long-term projects or set strategy. The best *Disruptors* have a tight-knit team, but also prioritize carving out an adequate amount of "personal time" to test ideas. Salman Khan's personal "hobby," creating math videos for his cousin on YouTube, turned into an international nonprofit that is "flipping the classroom" by changing when and how students learn and interact with teachers and educational institutions.

3. **Build open platforms on which problems can be solved.** When you are tackling a big challenge, design the problem in a way that lets many people pitch in to solve it. In a matter of ten days, 60,000 *Foldit* gamers were able to do what biochemists had been trying to do for a decade: they deciphered the structure of a protein called retroviral protease, an enzyme that is key to the way HIV multiplies.

Words to Live By:

> *"If you obey all the rules, you miss all the fun."*[10]
>
> —Katharine Hepburn

CONNECTIONAL INTELLIGENCE QUIZ

HOW CONNECTIONALLY INTELLIGENT AM I?

On the next page are five questions based on the 5 C's of Connectional Intelligence. Think about your behaviors in a specific role—at home as a parent, spouse, sibling, roommate or friend; at work as a manager or teammate; or in the community as a leader or volunteer. In this role, how often do you use the 5 C's? Rate yourself from 1(lowest) to 4 (highest) on each question based on what best describes your behavior. Or ask your teammates or others to rate how connectionally intelligent you are in your role, using the 5 C's. The value of this assessment depends entirely on your willingness to respond openly and honestly.

Note: The maximum number of points you can receive is 16. Why can't you earn a 20 if there are five categories? The maximum of 16 is intentional. The point of the quiz is to identify the C's that you are strongest in and to be honest about your weaknesses. So if you rate yourself a four in both Curiosity and Combination, for example, you will have eight points remaining to use in the categories of Combustion, Courage and Community. Every person has more strengths in some of the C's than in others. Choose your rating carefully, based on where your strengths lie.

In my current role as _____ :

QUIZ

Question	Rating

#1. Curiosity
How well am I framing and asking different questions from different contexts to gain new perspectives?

#2. Combination
How well am I taking different ideas, resources or products and combining them to create new concepts, new ways of thinking and surprising results?

#3. Community
How well am I bringing people together to create, spark new ideas and develop care and understanding?

#4. Courage
How well am I sparking and engaging in diverse and difficult conversations, even in the face of uncertainty and fear, and keeping these ideas and connections alive and amplifying them?

#5. Combustion
How well am I mobilizing and igniting diverse networks to activate and create change?

REFLECTION ON YOUR QUIZ RESULTS

The following scoring legend will give you an idea how strongly you are using connectional intelligence in your role:

13–16 = Outstanding! Continue dreaming, enabling, connecting and executing!

9–12 = Good. You're on the right track.

5–8 = Getting there. Focus on your strengths and become aware of your weaknesses.

Take a look at your scores and reflect on the following questions:

1. In which attributes (5 C's) did you score highest? These are your strengths.
    - Write down some examples of how you use these attributes in the role you defined.
    - Write down some concrete actions you can take to leverage your strengths. This may involve connecting with people who need to leverage your strengths.
    - Write down some actions you can take so you can continue to build upon these strengths. Many times it is better to be an expert in one or two of the C's than to be perfect on all dimensions.

2. In which attributes (5 C's) did you score lowest? These are your areas of opportunity.
    - Write down some examples of how you use these attributes in the role you defined.
    - Write down some concrete actions you can take to improve your use of these attributes in your role.
    - Write down some concrete actions you can take to mitigate these weaknesses. This typically involves connecting with people who score well on these attributes and can fill your gaps.

3. Did your results surprise you? Why? How can you leverage the results in your role?
    - Write down which of the 5 C's are most important to use in order to be particularly successful in your role.

MAPPING YOUR RESULTS BACK
TO THE CXQ ROLE MODELS

When assessing your strengths across the 5 C's, notice if your results align your chosen CxQ role model. If you have high curiosity in your role, are you a *Seeker* or a *Dreamer?* If you have high courage in your role, are you an *Advocate* or an *Adventurer?* Maybe you have high combustion—are you a *Disruptor* or an *Activist?* Notice how you might use the 5 C's differently based on the roles you take.

When assessing your weaknesses across the 5 C's, we urge you think about how you can partner or work with specific CxQ role models whose CxQ complements yours, raising your CxQ and allowing you, together, to get big things done.

Here are some CxQ role models you might want to partner with to improve your score on the 5 C's. Circle the CxQ role models you might like to consider.

TABLE 2

To raise your . . .	Partner with these CxQ role models . . .
Curiosity	Seekers
	Dreamers
	Adventurers
Combination	Mix Masters
	Empathetic Entrepreneurs
	Creative Company Individuals
Community	Activists
	Advocates
	Inspired Leaders
	Creative Company Individuals
Courage	Dreamers
	Adventurers
	Advocates
	Activists
Combustion	Disruptors
	Activists
	Empathetic Entrepreneurs
	Mix Masters

Make a list of people in your life and work out who can take on the roles you circled. Learn from them. Take them out to coffee, work with them on a special project, or study what they do well. Together, you can get big things done and fill in your gaps across the 5 C's with other CxQ role models.

GET BIG THINGS DONE WORK PLAN

This five-step plan requires you to write things down, clearly stating your vision, identifying what you don't know well and articulating what you believe. Write in this book. This plan will give you the power to cross the line, step-by-step, and get big things done.

> *"You are more likely to act your way into a new way of thinking than to think your way into a new way of acting."*[11]
>
> —Richard Pascale

1. **What's the big thing you want to get done?**

   This is your big goal, the dream you want to supersize using connectional intelligence for your work or life.

2. **Why does it matter?**

   Why does it matter to you? Why might it matter to other constituencies (networks, people, groups) who are trying to get the same thing done? Why might it matter to people you aren't connected to yet?

3. **Who are all the people and groups you can leverage to get this big thing done?**

   Who does this big thing really matter to that you can leverage? Does it matter to your stakeholders? Does it matter to the people you are trying to serve? Does it matter to anyone else?

4. **How can you activate your connectional intelligence to get this big thing done?**

> How can you involve everyone who can help? How can you work with key influencers, gatekeepers and authorities? What types of resources and ideas can you leverage? How can you use different tools and technologies to turn your ideas to action? How can you connect with new people and networks to tackle the big thing you want to get done? How can you go to improbable places and to unlikely people to find solutions?

5. **Action List:** List every task that needs to happen, by whom and when to get your big thing done.

> Write down which of the 5 C's and CxQ role models you will need to most frequently employ in your tasks.

GET BIG THINGS DONE
MANAGER GUIDE

Whether you're the CEO of a Fortune 500 company or managing a team of interns at a start-up, you can help raise the connectional intelligence of all your team members. Here is a team exercise to begin pulling your team out of the past and into the brighter world of connectional intelligence.

Purpose of exercise: To give team members a forum for providing one another with focused, direct and actionable feedback about how their individual connectional intelligence can improve the performance of the team; and to define a project in which the team needs to leverage connectional intelligence.

Time required: One or two hours, depending on the size of the team and the skill of the facilitator.

Instructions:
1. **Take the Connectional Intelligence Quiz.** Have each team member complete the Connectional Intelligence Quiz on their own. Next, as a group, the team can complete a quiz for each member based on the role he or she plays in the group.

2. **Tally your individual and team results.** When completed, ask each team member to tally up their personal score and the score

they received from team members. Ask each team member to identify a top strength and top weakness across the 5 C's, using the quiz results.

(Note: Team members should write down their answers so that they can commit to and remember their responses, and are not tempted to change the responses based on what others have said about them.)

3. **Share your results.** Beginning with comments from the manager of the team, have all team members read their strengths and weaknesses aloud, one by one, until everyone has finished. Accumulate the total team score for strengths and weaknesses across the 5 C's on a whiteboard.

    Discuss the results on the whiteboard with the team, using the following questions:

    - What is your single most important C that contributes to the strength of the team? (That is, their strength.)
    - What is your single most important C that limits the strength of the team? (That is, a weakness or development opportunity.)
    - What do you think is the most important C to do well as a team to accomplish the team's goal?

4. **Ask the team leader to respond to what people have said.** Identify the gaps that exist across the 5 C's among the whole team and have a discussion about how to best work on these areas. Maybe there is low curiosity across your team. If so, you might want to spend more time broadening perspectives before you solve problems. Or perhaps there is low courage; you may desire to host mini "sparring" sessions to inspire, provoke and share diverse opinions. Or maybe you realize you need more combustion and you need to start connecting and activating

deeper client networks or cross-disciplinary groups to spark change.

5. **Identify your CxQ role models.** Map the CxQ role models across your team based on the quiz results. Have each team member choose one CxQ role model that best describes his or her strength on the team based on quiz results. You may be playing different CxQ role models at different times, so choose the CxQ role model that you may be playing in your specific role on the team. (See Table 3.)

6. **Accumulate the total team CxQ role models and notice the gaps across the team across the three categories of CxQ role models:** *Thinkers, Enablers* **and** *Connection Executors.*

    For every team, you need the right balance of the three categories of CxQ role models: *Thinkers* who help spark and generate the big ideas, *Enablers* who create the structures and forces to get big things done, and *Connection Executors* who mobilize others to get big things done.

    Do you have more *Thinkers* than *Connection Executors?* Or is your team filled up with *Enablers?* Notice commonalities and opportunities for individuals with different CxQ role models to partner with one another on the team or outside the team to get big things done. (See Table 4.)

7. **Fill out the** *"Get Big Things Done"* **Work Plan as a team.** Choose one or two specific projects your team is trying to get done and answer the questions about how you can leverage connectional intelligence.

8. **Design a next steps action plan based on your work in Step 7.** Make a plan designed to improve the connectional intelligence attributes across your team and to encourage the

TABLE 3

If your strength was . . .	You might be one of these . . .
Curiosity	Seekers
	Dreamers
	Adventurers
Combination	Mix Masters
	Empathetic Entrepreneurs
	Creative Company Individuals
Community	Activists
	Advocates
	Inspired Leaders
	Creative Company Individuals
Courage	Dreamers
	Adventurers
	Advocates
	Activists
Combustion	Disruptors
	Activists
	Empathetic Entrepreneurs
	Mix Masters

TABLE 4

Thinkers	Enablers	Connection Executors
Dreamers	Inspired Leaders	Mix Masters
Adventurers	Advocates	Activists
Seekers	Creative Company	Disruptors
	Individuals	Empathetic Entrepreneurs

right mix of CxQ role model partnerships to get big things done. Once you know the team strengths and weaknesses across the 5 C's and the CxQ role models that show up on your team, answer the following questions in a team action plan:

  a. Of the 5 C's, which attributes can we improve as a whole team?

   b. How can we partner different skill sets within our team to fill our gaps across the 5 C's (e.g., matching *Dreamers* with *Mix Masters, Activists* with *Creative Company Individuals*)?

   c. Is there someone, not on the team, who could help fill our gaps across the three categories of CxQ role models (e.g., *Thinkers, Enablers* and *Connection Executors*)?

   d. Are there other individuals, groups or crowds we can reach to fill in CxQ role models we are missing (e.g., industry associations, cross-disciplinary conferences, digital communities, crowd-sourcing platforms, CEOs, entrepreneurs)?

   e. What are three practical actions we can take to improve our connectional intelligence as a team?

9. **Track takeaways and next steps.** When all team members have received input from their peers, have each person summarize aloud for the team the one or two key action takeaways that he or she will work on individually and with others on the team. Have them e-mail those takeaways to the manager.

GET BIG THINGS DONE REALLY GOOD NEWS: INSPIRING THOUGHTS

Reflection is a critical starting point in building your connectional intelligence. Here are a set of statements designed to spur reflection and reveal important facets of how you are using your connectional intelligence to get big things done.

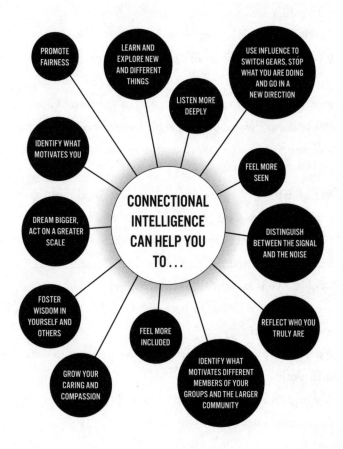

GET BIG THINGS DONE READING
GROUP DISCUSSION GUIDE

Now that you've read this book, it's time to go out and debate these ideas with your community, on your blog or on a social networking site. If you really want to bring these ideas to life, talk them over in person with colleagues from work, friends at school, or your book club. Connectional intelligence starts conversation by conversation.

1. In what aspects of your life and work do you think you're connectionally intelligent? Are you using connectional intelligence in some situations and not in others? Give examples.

2. What about the important people in your lives—your partners, colleagues, your friends, your kids—how would you rate their CxQ?

3. Which parts of *Get Big Things Done* resonated most strongly with you? Were there parts you disagreed with—and why?

4. Can you think of a time in your life when using connectional intelligence proved to be an advantage? Disadvantage?

5. Who are your favorite CxQ role models?

6. Do you agree with the authors that CxQ is a key attribute of today's leaders?

7. Are you an introvert or extrovert? How do you use CxQ differently?

8. If you're an introvert, what do you find most challenging about connecting intelligently with extroverts?

9. If you're an extrovert, what do you find most challenging about connecting intelligently with introverts?

10. If you're not a "tech person," what do you find most challenging and most rewarding about using connectional intelligence?

11. If you are a "tech person" what do you find most challenging and most rewarding about using connectional intelligence?

12. *Get Big Things Done* suggests that connectional intelligence is not about technology or tools, but more about unleashing human connection. Have you experienced the difference between technology and human connection in your own workplace?

13. Do you think your job enables your connectional intelligence? If not, what could you do to grow your CxQ?

14. (If you have children) How does your connectional intelligence compare to that of your children? How can you improve your relationships by relating to them differently?

15. (If you're in a relationship) How does your connectional intelligence compare to that of your partner? How do you handle areas in which you're not compatible?

16. Do you enjoy social media such as Facebook and Twitter? Do you like using connectional intelligence with tools and technologies?

17. Can you think of a time in your life when being disconnected from networks proved to be more connectionally intelligent for you?

18. What is the #1 thing you think CxQ can change in the world?

GET BIG THINGS DONE RECAP

This book has covered a lot of ground—and you might not be able to instantly recall everything in it. So here you'll find the definition of connectional intelligence, a GBTD Twitter summary, coffee shop talking points and your refresher course.

Definition:

Connectional intelligence is the ability to combine the world's diversity of people, networks, disciplines and resources, forging connections that create value, meaning and breakthrough results.

Twitter Summary:

#GBTD shows that connectional intelligence is the key to success and leadership in the world today.

Connectional Intelligence is the monster wave of our time—we're all riding it together. #gbtd

IQ and EQ are so last century. For 21st century we need to upgrade and use our connectional intelligence (CxQ) to get big things done #gbtd

Coffee Shop Summary:

First things first. What is connectional intelligence or CxQ?

Put simply, we define CxQ as the capacity to derive value and meaning from familiar and far-flung networks of people, ideas and knowledge.

Why does it matter?

Connectional intelligence is a force multiplier; it's the confidence to navigate a universe in which we may all accomplish more than we ever dared to imagine by drawing on the almost limitless supply of our collective brain power, heart power and material resources.

Why now?

Connectional intelligence is unleashing its vast powers now because this is the first time in history that billions of people are *inclusively* connected— to each other, to all of the world's knowledge, to different points of view, to instant news, music, culture and health.

GBTD Refresher Course:

Here's your GBTD chapter-by-chapter summary.

PART ONE

Chapter 1

The Big Wave

What is connectional intelligence and where do we see it at work in the world? (The answer: everywhere.) How is it changing the lives of individuals and groups in business, sports, academics and politics? And most importantly, how do we harness this connectional intelligence to get us to the places we want to go?

Chapter 2

The Roots of Connectional Intelligence

This is the first time in history that billions of people have been inclusively connected. In this chapter, we explore the historical roots of connectional intelligence when people's connections and spheres of influence were limited by time and location. We explore the essential questions that have always been at the center of connectional intelligence:

Why? What if? Does it matter? How? And we see that today we are moving past Malcolm Gladwell's "law of the few" to the "connected potential of many."

PART TWO
Chapter 3
How to Get Big Things Done: A Primer
This chapter explores the topography of connectional intelligence in the modern world: how a pumpkin farmer in Rhode Island is changing agricultural practices in India; how a group of first-year law associates created a highly efficient social media treasure trove of legal genius; how a twenty-year-old Vietnamese immigrant, working as a waitress to put herself through school, used her MacBook Pro to revolutionize the cosmetics industry; and how Khan Academy is creating a powerful inversion in teaching and learning, changing the future of modern education.

Chapter 4
Connect Intelligently
The traditional routes to power—the schools you go to, the contacts in your address book, the families you are born to—are no longer the only ways to get ahead. In an ever-shifting digital landscape where fortune favors the brave, the quick and the connectionally intelligent, how do you get big things done? We look at models of connectional intelligence success at companies, big and small, including: Colgate, Quirky, Mitticool, Honey Bee Network, Nike, MIT Little Devices, Oreo and KLM.

Chapter 5
Courage Builds on Courage
Connectional intelligence isn't just about winning big in business or pursuing a big, ambitious, creative dream. More and more, people are

using technology and their own connectional intelligence to respond within minutes and hours to natural disasters, to the violent aftermath of political events and to terrorist acts. We look at powerful and inspiring examples from relief efforts after the earthquake in Haiti to helping teens in crisis. Courage builds on courage: this is where connectional intelligence really goes big. Something you read in this book could help you use your own connectional intelligence when a future calamity strikes.

Chapter 6
Connect and Make Change

Connectional intelligence dramatically amps the reach and influence of individuals. In this chapter, we look at how connectional intelligence helped seemingly average individuals to, literally, change their world. We'll look at many stories, including those of a scientist who is using virtual-reality games to lower pain for burn victims, a nine-year-old school girl whose protests about unhealthy lunches sparked a national debate about nutrition that amplified into a nonprofit she funds, and we'll meet grandmothers in England who, through connectivity and caring, make meaning in their own lives by mentoring slum children in India—playing a critically important role in the lives of young people who in another era they would have never had the opportunity to touch.

Chapter 7
Problem Solving and the Power of Play

One of the most potent forms of connectional intelligence is how innovative individuals are designing problems in a way that attracts people to pitch in to solve them. Digital games have emerged as a powerful platform for connectional intelligence because the ability to process data quickly, make connections and solve problems are all hardwired into the DNA of the gaming culture. We'll look at stories, ranging from language-learning, to waste cleanup to solving science problems, that are engaging record-breaking numbers of people in seemingly simple tasks that ultimately address real-world challenges.

Chapter 8
The Power of Difference

One of the things that makes connectional intelligence such a force for good is that it allows people to come together, while standing strong in what makes them unique. In other words, this chapter is about the connectional intelligence of freaks, geeks and other proud outsiders. We'll be looking at the evolution of music superstar Pharrell and his powerful geek-supporting youth campaign, "i am OTHER," Deloitte's "Uncovering" diversity program, and *The Fault in Our Stars* author John Green and his powerful, inspiring, thousands-strong crew of Nerdfighters.

Chapter 9
Why Not? Reimagining What's Possible

In this chapter, we meet people who are changing the face of health care and education, whose solutions are affecting our present and our futures. We will also meet several modern-day adventurers, who, in their quest to get big things done, are connecting to answer some of the most pressing environmental problems of our time.

PART THREE
Pulling It All Together
Your Get Big Things Done Handbook

Now that you've read about the many ways connectional intelligence can be used to get big things done, how do you apply it to your own life? Here we dive in and focus on how you can use what we've presented in this book to make practical and powerful changes in your own life and work. Since there are as many ways to be connectionally intelligent as there are people, we're offering up several different ways to work with this material.

- 5 C's of Connectional Intelligence
- CxQ Role Models
- Connectional Intelligence Quiz
- *Get Big Things Done* Work Plan
- *Get Big Things Done* Manager Guide
- *Get Big Things Done* Really Good News
- *Get Big Things Done* Reading Discussion Guide

ACKNOWLEDGMENTS

THIS BOOK COULD NOT HAVE BEEN WRITTEN WITHOUT THE generosity of hundreds of people who have assisted us along the way.

First and foremost, we would like to thank the many people we interviewed in organizations and communities across the globe and the extensive list of leaders who agreed to be interviewed for this book. Their insights, struggles and leadership have taught and inspired us.

Special thanks to Veronica Chambers for her vision, commitment, wisdom and generous partnership on the journey. This book is immeasurably better for her extensive contributions. Thanks also to all the members of our team, including: Jesse Kornbluth, Peter Smith, Doug Reynolds, Lena Goodwin and Corinne Lippie.

Jim Levine understood the promise of this book and believed in us every inch of the way. We are grateful to have him as our literary agent, guide and friend.

Emily Carleton, Laurie Harting, Lauren Janiec, Christine Catarino, Alan Bradshaw and many others at Palgrave Macmillan have been a wonderful team to work with. The book is better for their efforts and guidance.

We are deeply grateful to our colleagues and friends for their belief in our work and their steadfast support of our efforts: Janet Abrahm, Fred Allen, April Anderson, Don Arnousde, Johan Aurik, Lotte Bailyn,

Gina Barnett, Damon Beyer, Beth Bovis, Kolina Cicero, Evann Clingan, Susan Crile, Kim Davis, Deb Dehaas, Rich Demato, Ron Donovan, James Elbaor, Walt Fey, Chelsea Finger, Marshall Ganz, Nicole Granet, Rahaf Harfoush, Jessica Harrison, Christine Hassler, Kate Hensley, Andrew Kaplan, Ajay Kapoor, Bharat Kapoor, Donna Kavjian, Jon Kessler, Anish Koshy, Alyson Krueger, Karim Lakhani, Sam Lam, Tammie Lay, Minsun Lee, Julie Lee, Ellen Levy, Daniel Mahler, Mackenzie Mallory, Arun Mathew, Bob Mauceri, Geraldine Moriba, Mana Nakagawa, Jeremy Neuner, Jacqueline Novogratz, Lisa Paragois, Tony Pino, Samantha Pitts-Kiefer, Alyson Potenza, Stephanie Rogen, Otto Scharmer, Dan Schawbel, Brad Schiller, Alicia Simons, Puneet Singh, Christie Smith, Tammy Smith, Andrew Stern, David Sutphen, Danielle Taylor, Lisa Wheeler, Steven Wolfe Pereira, Aaron Wolff, Candice Yee, Leslie Zaikis and Randi Zeller.

Thank you to communities who have supported our work: AT-Kearney, CNN, Levo League, HQ, Young Entrepreneur Council, Harvard Kennedy School, Summit Series and the World Economic Forum Global Shapers.

Finally, for their love, encouragement, and patience as we devoted so much time and energy to this book, we would like to thank our families. For Saj-nicole: Saj-nicole's parents, Daniel and Thelma; and Kathy, Carol-Anne, Steve, Clifford, Darlene, Eric, Janelle, Stephanie, Liz and Alicia. For Erica: her husband, Rahul; her parents, Ram and Neelam and Abha and Krishan; and Darpun, Rohit, Neil, Malavika, Angela, Vijay, Rishi and Aristu.

NOTES

CHAPTER 1

1. Vannevar Bush, "As We May Think," *The Atlantic Monthly,* July 1, 1945, http://www.theatlantic.com/magazine/archive/1945/07/as-we-may-think/303881/.
2. Ali Heriyanto, "This Is What Happened When We Called Quirky's Least Important CEO," *Chipchick,* June 30, 2014, http://www.chipchick.com/2014/06/happened-called-quirky-least-important-ceo.html.
3. Ariel Schwartz, "Nike Launches GreenXchange for Corporate Idea-Sharing," *Fast Company,* February 3, 2010, http://www.fastcompany.com/1536739/nike-launches-greenxchange-corporate-idea-sharing.
4. Sheila Shayon, "My Starbucks Idea Turns 5, Sparking a Latte Revolution," *Brandchannel,* April 1, 2013, http://www.brandchannel.com/home/post/2013/04/01/MyStarbucks-Idea-Turns-5-040113.aspx.
5. John Hagel III, John Seely Brown and Lang Davidson, *The Power of Pull: How Small Moves, Smartly Made, Can Set Big Things in Motion* (New York: Basic Books, 2010), 1-23.
6. Joseph Campbell, *The Hero with a Thousand Faces* (Novato: New World Library, 2008).
7. Ibid., 196.

CHAPTER 2

1. Sir Edward Cook, *The Life of Florence Nightingale* (London: Macmillan and Co., 1913), 254.
2. I. Bernard Cohen, "Florence Nightingale," http://www.unc.edu/~nielsen/soci708/cdocs/cohen.htm.
3. Cook, *The Life of Florence Nightingale,* 387.
4. Mark Bostridge, "Florence Nightingale: The Lady with the Lamp," *BBC,* February 17, 2011, http://www.bbc.co.uk/history/british/victorians/nightingale_01.shtml.
5. Fox Butterfield, "From Ben Franklin, A Gift That's Worth Two Fights," *The New York Times,* April 21, 1990, http://www.nytimes.com/1990/04/21/us/from-ben-franklin-a-gift-that-s-worth-two-fights.html.

6. Carl Van Doren, *Benjamin Franklin* (New York: Penguin Books, 1991), 763.

7. Warren Berger, *A More Beautiful Question: The Power of Inquiry to Spark Breakthrough Ideas,* (New York: Bloomsbury, 2006), 4.

8. Warren Berger, "How to Cultivate the Art of Asking Good Questions," *The Wall Street Journal,* March 5, 2014, http://blogs.wsj.com/speakeasy/2014/03/05/how-to-cultivate-the-art-of-asking-good-questions/.

9. Malcolm Gladwell, *The Tipping Point* (New York: Little Brown, 2000), 33.

10. Ibid.

11. Florence Nightingale, *Florence Nightingale on Mysticism and Eastern Religion,* ed. Gérard Vallée (Ontario: Wilfrid Laurier University Press, 2003), 260.

12. Joe Dolce, "When Yotam Met Sami," *Gourmet,* February 2009, http://www.gourmet.com/magazine/2000s/2009/02/yotam-ottolenghi-profile.

13. Edward Morgan Forrester, *Howard's End* (New York: Bedford Books, 1997), 409.

14. Bülent Atalay and Keith Wamsley, *Leonardo's Universe: The Renaissance World of Leonardo DaVinci* (New York: National Geographic, 2009), 96.

CHAPTER 3

1. Billy Baker, "Man Grows First One Ton Pumpkin," *Boston Globe,* September 28, 2012, http://www.bostonglobe.com/metro/2012/09/28/man-grows-first-one-ton-pumpkin/4G7p98dDirbbHMEQazd7TN/story.html.

2. Ron Wallace, in a phone interview with the authors, March 13, 2013.

3. Baker, "Man Grows First One Ton Pumpkin."

4. Ron Wallace, in a phone interview with the authors, March 13, 2013.

5. Catherine Rampell, "They Did Their Homework, 800 Years of It," *The New York Times,* July 4, 2010, http://www.nytimes.com/2010/07/04/business/economy/04econ.html?pagewanted=all.

6. Ruth Alexander, "Reinhart, Rogoff . . . and Herndon: The Student Who Caught Out the Profs," *BBC,* April 19, 2013, http://www.bbc.com/news/magazine-22223190.

7. Ibid.

8. Thomas Herndon, Michael Ash, Robert Pollin, "Does High Public Debt Consistently Stifle Economic Growth? A Critique of Reinhart and Rogoff," *Political Economy Research Institute,* April 15, 2013, http://www.peri.umass.edu/236/hash/31e2ff374b6377b2ddec04deaa6388b1/publication/566/.

9. Center for Economic and Policy Research, "How Much Unemployment was Caused by Reinhart and Rogoff's Arithmetic Mistake?" April 16, 2013, http://www.cepr.net/index.php/blogs/beat-the-press/how-much-unemployment-was-caused-by-reinhart-and-rogoffs-arithmetic-mistake.

10. Edward Krudy, "How a Student Took on Eminent Economists on Debt Issues and Won," *Reuters,* April 18, 2013, http://www.reuters.com/article/2013/04/18/us-global-economy-debt-herndon-idUSBRE93H0CV20130418.

11. Jay Fitzgerald, "Student's Critique of Austerity Policies Creates Firestorm," *The Boston Globe,* June 22, 2013, http://www.bostonglobe.com/business/2013/06/22/igniting-firestorm-over-austerity-policies/fZbc78sfvAOiJGBDPEgALL/story.html.

12. Alexander, "Reinhart, Rogoff . . . and Herndon."
13. Paul Krugman, "The Conscience of a Liberal," *The New York Times,* April 16, 2013, http://krugman.blogs.nytimes.com/page/55/?nl=todaysheadlines&emc=edit_ae_20120319.
14. *Economics One Blog,* "Coding Errors, Austerity and Exploding Debt," blog entry by John B. Taylor, April 22, 2010, http://economicsone.com/2013/04/22/coding-errors-austerity-and-exploding-debt/.
15. *The Big Wave Blog,* "History," http://www.thebigwaveblog.com/big-wave-surfing-history.
16. Ibid.
17. Sumeet Moghe, "The Power of Pull—John Seely Brown," *The Learning Generalist,* November 2, 2010, http://www.learninggeneralist.com/2010/11/power-of-pull-john-seely-brown.html.
18. Linda Tucci, "Leaving the Past Behind and Embracing the 'New Normal' in IT," *TechTarget,* July 28, 2010, http://searchcio.techtarget.com/news/1517420/Leaving-the-past-behind-and-embracing-the-new-normal-in-IT.
19. Hilary Howard, "Telling Stories, Selling Beauty," *The New York Times,* August 7, 2013, http://www.nytimes.com/2013/08/08/fashion/telling-stories-selling-beauty.html?pagewanted=1&_r=0&adxnnl=1&ref=todayspaper&adxnnlx=1408967198-U%20T17ULhFNbzROzB44TKwA.
20. "YouTube Makeup Guru on Becoming a Beauty Superstar," *Glamour,* September 2013, http://www.glamour.com/lipstick/2013/09/michelle-phan-youtube-beauty-glamour-october-2013.
21. Stephanie Hayes, "Michelle Phan, a YouTube Sensation for her Makeup Tutorials, Has Transformed Her Life," *Tampa Bay Times,* August 22, 2009, http://www.tampabay.com/features/humaninterest/michelle-phan-a-youtube-sensation-for-her-makeup-tutorials-has-transformed/1029747.
22. Michelle Phan, "Video," http://michellephan.com/category/video/.
23. Michelle Phan, "About Me," http://michellephan.com/about-me/.
24. Rachel Strutgatz, "VLoggers Winning Online Battle Over Brands," *WWD,* March 14, 2014, http://www.wwd.com/media-news/media-features/vloggers-winning-online-battle-over-brands-7592082.
25. Eva Chen, "Video Exclusive: Michelle Phan for Lancome Holiday Makeup How-To," *Teen Vogue,* November 22, 2010, http://www.teenvogue.com/blog/teen-vogue-daily/2010/11/michelle-phan.html.
26. Alison Beard, "Life's Work: Salman Khan," *Harvard Business Review,* January 2014, http://hbr.org/2014/01/salman-khan/ar/1.
27. Michael Noer, "One Man, One Computer, 10 Million Students," *Forbes,* November 2, 2012, http://www.forbes.com/sites/michaelnoer/2012/11/02/one-man-one-computer-10-million-students-how-khan-academy-is-reinventing-education.
28. Salman Khan, "Let's Use Video to Reinvent Education," TED, March 2011, https://www.ted.com/talks/salman_khan_let_s_use_video_to_reinvent_education/transcript.
29. Ibid.
30. Ibid.

CHAPTER 4

1. "Colgate-Palmolive," *Forbes,* http://www.forbes.com/companies/colgate-palmo live/.
2. "Method to Get Fluoride Powder into Toothpaste Tubes," *Idea Connection,* http://www.ideaconnection.com/open-innovation-success/Method-to-Get-Flu oride-Powder-into-Toothpaste-Tubes-00057.html.
3. Jeff Howe, "The Rise of Crowdsourcing," *Wired,* June 2006, http://archive .wired.com/wired/archive/14.06/crowds.html.
4. Ed Melcarek, "'From a 'Jack to a King,' a True Story," *Innocentive,* August 20, 2008, http://www.innocentive.com/blog/2008/08/20/ed-melcarek/.
5. Ibid.
6. Ibid.
7. Ibid.
8. US Chamber Foundation, "Millennial Generation Research Review," National Chamber Foundation, 2012, http://www.uschamberfoundation.org /millennial-generation-research-review.
9. Carmen Nobel, "Colgate Seeks Fresh Ideas in Personal Care," *The Street,* May 4, 2010, http://www.thestreet.com/story/10744025/1/colgate-seeks-fresh-ideas-in -personal-care.html.
10. Josh Dean, "Is This the World's Most Creative Manufacturer?," *Inc.,* October 2013, http://www.inc.com/magazine/201310/josh-dean/is-quirky-the-worlds-m ost-creative-manufacturer.html
11. Natt Garun, "How Social Community Shapes and Develops Quirky Products," *Digital Trends,* July 30, 2012, http://www.digitaltrends.com/home/how -social-community-shapes-and-develop-quirky-products/#!bJNnSI.
12. Joshua Brustein, "Why GE Sees Big Things in Quirky's Little Inventions," *Businessweek,* November 13, 2013, http://www.businessweek.com/articles/2013-11-13 /why-ge-sees-big-things-in-quirkys-little-inventions.
13. Eliza Brooke, "Quirky, The New York-Based Invention Machine, Brings On Doreen Lorenzo as President to Build Out Product Categories," *TechCrunch,* October 1, 2013, http://techcrunch.com/2013/10/01/quirky-the-new-york-bas ed-invention-machine-brings-on-doreen-lorenzo-as-president-to-build-out- product-categories/.
14. Dean, "Is This the World's Most Creative Manufacturer?"
15. Vivek Sinha, "Mitticool: Son of the Soil Keeps Things Cool with His 'Desi Gadget,'" *Hindustan Times,* January 14, 2014, http://www.hindustantimes.com /india-news/mitticool-son-of-the-soil-keeps-things-cool-with-his-desi-gadget /article1-1172621.aspx.
16. Navi Radjou, Jaideep Prabhu, Simone Ahuja and Kevin Roberts, *Jugaad Innovation: Think Frugal, Be Flexible, Generate Breakthroughs* (New York: Jossey-Bass, 2012).
17. Anil Gupta, "India's Hidden Hotbeds of Innovation." TED, November 2009, https://www.ted.com/talks/anil_gupta_india_s_hidden_hotbeds_of_inven tion.
18. Ariel Schwartz, "Nike Launches GreenXchange for Corporate Idea-Sharing," *Fast Company,* February 3, 2010, http://www.fastcompany.com/1536739/nike -launches-greenxchange-corporate-idea-sharing.

19. Don Tapscott, "Davos and Partners Launch the GreenXchange," *Businessweek,* January 27, 2010, http://www.businessweek.com/the_thread/techbeat/archives /2010/01/davos_nike_and.html.

20. Nike, "Nike Releases Environmental Design Tool," November 29, 2010, http:// nikeinc.com/news/nike-releases-environmental-design-tool-to-industry.

21. "How Nike's Green Design Saved 82 Million Plastic Bottles," *Greenbiz,* February 9, 2011, http://www.greenbiz.com/blog/2011/02/09/how-nikes-green -design-saved-82m-plastic-bottles.

22. Little Devices @ MIT, "Little Devices, Big Ideas," http://littledevices.org/.

23. David Chandler, "In the World: MIT-designed Cooler Preserves Tuberculosis Drugs; Record Doses," *MIT News,* http://newsoffice.mit.edu/2012/fighting -tuberculosis-0530.

24. Tina Rosenburg, "Playing with Toys and Saving Lives," *The New York Times,* January 29, 2014, http://opinionator.blogs.nytimes.com/2014/01/29/playing -with-toys-and-saving-lives/.

25. Ibid.

26. B. Bonin Bough, "The Power of Real-Time Advertising," *Harvard Business Review,* February 5, 2013, http://blogs.hbr.org/2013/02/the-power-of-real-time-ad verti/.

27. "Who Bought What in Superbowl XLVIII," *AdAge,* February 3, 2014, http:// adage.com/article/special-report-super-bowl/super-bowl-ad-chart-buying-super -bowl-2014/244024/.

28. Thomas Barrabi, "Is the Superbowl Fixed? Rumors that NFL, BookMakers Rig Game Persist, Cite XLVII Power Outage as Proof," *International Business Times,* January 31, 2014, http://www.ibtimes.com/super-bowl-fixed-rumors-nfl-book makers-rig-game-persist-cite-xlvii-power-outage-proof-1549788.

29. Dave Smith, "Why the Best Super Bowl Ad in 2013 Was Free," *International Business Times,* February 4, 2014, http://www.ibtimes.com/why-best-super-bowl -ad-2013-was-free-1059500.

30. 360i, "The Oreo Blackout Tweet," http://www.360i.com/work/oreo-super-bowl/.

31. Rob Bleaney, "KLM Sombrero Tweet Mocking Mexico's World Cup Exit to Holland Causes Fury," *The Guardian,* June 30, 2014, http://www.theguard ian.com/football/2014/jun/30/klm-sobrero-tweet-mexico-world-cup-holland -gael-garcia-bernal.

32. Ibid.

CHAPTER 5

1. Ory Okolloh, "Ory Okolloh: How I Became an Activist," TED, August 2008, https://www.ted.com/talks/ory_okolloh_on_becoming_an_activist/transcript.

2. Josias Gassesse, "Ory Okolloh: The Kenyan Queen of Digital in Africa!," *Africa Top Success,* March 21, 2014, http://www.africatopsuccess.com/en/2014/03/21 /ory-okolloh-the-kenyan-queen-of-digital-in-africa/.

3. Richard Longhurst, "Famines, Food and Nutrition: Issues and Opportunities for Policy and Research," http://archive.unu.edu/unupress/food/8F091e/8F091E05 .htm.

4. Kenyan Pundit, "About," http://www.kenyanpundit.com/about/.

5. Ushahidi, "Frequently Asked Questions," http://www.ushahidi.com/mission/faq/.

6. Russ Linden, "The Life-Saving Power of Crowdsourcing," *Governing,* January 23, 2013, http://www.governing.com/columns/mgmt-insights/col-crowd wourcing-ushahidi-saving-lives-haiti-earthquake.html.

7. Ibid.

8. Ibid.

9. Ohuud Saad, "Tahrir Supplies: A Superhero Has Finally Landed," *What Women Want Magazine,* January 2012, http://whatwomenwant-mag.com/2012/12/tahrir-supplies-a-superhero-has-finaly-landed/.

10. Ibid.

11. Ibid.

12. Interzone Rebels, "Requests and Needs from #Eqypt #Tahrir and #Elsewhere," *Storify,* https://storify.com/interzonerebels/requests-and-needs-from-egypt-tah rir-and-elsewhere.

13. Clive Thompson, *Smarter Than You Think: How Technology Is Changing Our Minds for the Better* (New York: Penguin Group, 2013), 156-7.

14. Ibid., 158.

15. McKinsey & Company, "The Improbable Story of Malala and McKinsey," http://www.mckinsey.com/careers/our_people_and_values/alumni-a_commu nity_for_life/the_improbable_story_of_malala_and_mckinsey.

16. Ibid.

17. Callie Schweitzer, "30 Under 30: Meet Shiza Shahid, Malala's Right-Hand Woman," *Time,* December 6, 2013, http://ideas.time.com/2013/12/06/30-under -30-shiza-shahid-and-the-malala-fund/.

18. Catupult, "Malala Fund," http://www.catapult.org/partners/partner/26675/public.

19. Do Something.org, "Campaigns," https://www.dosomething.org/campaigns.

20. Do Something.org, "Nancy Lublin: CEO & Chief Old Person," https://www.dosomething.org/staff/nancy_lublin.

21. Nancy Lublin, "Texting That Saves Lives," TED, April 2012, http://www.ted.com/talks/nancy_lublin_texting_that_saves_lives/transcript.

22. Ibid.

23. Naomi Hirabayashi, in a phone interview with the authors, June 26, 2014.

24. Ibid.

25. Lublin, "Texting That Saves Lives."

26. Naomi Hirabayashi, in a phone interview with the authors, June 26, 2014.

27. John H. Richardson, "Lance Armstrong in Purgatory: The Afterlife," *Esquire,* July 7, 2014, http://www.esquire.com/features/lance-armstrong-interview-0814.

28. Robert R. Wood, "Lance Armstrong Payback for Sunday Times 'Libel' That Wasn't," *Forbes,* August 27, 2013, http://www.forbes.com/sites/robertwood/2013/08/27/lance-armstrong-payback-for-sunday-times-libel-that-wasnt/.

29. Mary Pilon, "Armstrong Aide Talks of Doping and Price Paid," *The New York Times,* October 12, 2012, http://www.nytimes.com/2012/10/13/sports/cycling/lance-armstrong-aide-talks-of-doping-and-price-paid.html?pagewant ed=all&_r=0.

30. Ibid.

31. Austin Murphy, "Betsy Andreu Always Knew That Lance Armstrong Doped," *Sports Illustrated,* January 17, 2013, http://www.si.com/more-sports/2013/01/17/betsy-andreu-lance-armstrong.

32. Ibid.
33. Ibid.
34. Andy Shen, "Michael Ashenson," *NY Velocity,* April 3, 2009, http://nyvelocity .com/content/interviews/2009/michael-ashenden.
35. David Carr, "Chasing Lance Armstrong's Misdeeds from the Sidelines," *The New York Times,* October 29, 2012, http://www.nytimes.com/2012/10/29/bus iness/media/chasing-lance-armstrongs-misdeeds-from-the-sidelines.html?page wanted=all.
36. Richardson, "Lance Armstrong in Purgatory: The Afterlife."
37. "It's Payback Time, Lance! Armstrong Told to Return Every Penny of Prize Money Earned During Doping Years," *Mail Online,* October 26, 2012, http:// www.dailymail.co.uk/sport/othersports/article-2223628/Lance-Armstrong-or dered-pay-prize-money-won-doping.html.
38. Richardson, "Lance Armstrong in Purgatory: The Afterlife."
39. Simon Marks, "Somaly Mam Holy Saint (and Sinner) Sex Trafficking," *News-week,* May 30, 2014, http://www.newsweek.com/2014/05/30/somaly-mam-holy -saint-and-sinner-sex-trafficking-251642.html.
40. Ibid.
41. Katha Pollit, "Sex Trafficking Lies & Money: Lessons from the Somoly Mam Scandal," *The Nation,* June 4, 2012, http://www.thenation.com/article/180132 /sex-trafficking-lies-money-lessons-somaly-mam-scandal.
42. Marks, "Somaly Mam Holy Saint (and Sinner) of Sex Trafficking."
43. Ibid.
44. International Labor Organization, *ILO Global Estimate of Forced Labor: Results and Methodology,* 2012. International Labor Office, "A Global Alliance Against Forced Labor, Global Report under the Follow-up to the ILO Declaration on Fundamental Principles and Rights at Work," 2005, http://www.ilo.org/public /english/standards/relm/ilc/ilc93/pdf/rep-i-b.pdf.
45. Audre Lorde, *Sister Outsider: Essays and Speeches by Audre Lorde* (Berkeley, CA: Crossing Press, 2007), 110-114.

CHAPTER 6

1. HIT Lab, "VR Therapy for Spider Phobia," http://www.hitl.washington.edu /projects/exposure/.
2. Hunter Hoffman, in a phone interview with the authors, February 25, 2014.
3. Ibid.
4. Ibid.
5. Ibid.
6. Ibid.
7. Ibid.
8. Ibid.
9. Steve Hartman, "How Letters from Strangers Saved a Teen's Life," *CBS News,* March 8, 2013, http://www.cbsnews.com/news/how-letters-from-strangers-sav ed-a-teens-life/.
10. Karen Brocklebank, "A Victim of Bullying," *Letters for Noah,* http://www.let tersfornoah.com/about-noah.html.
11. Ibid.

12. Shelley Ng, "Mom's Inspirational Letter Drive Causes Bullied Maryland Boy to Retreat from Plan to Commit Suicide, Attracts 10,000 Messages from Kindhearted People Across the Globe," *The New York Daily News,* March 10, 2013, http://www.nydailynews.com/news/national/mom-inspirational-letter-drive -bullied-maryland-boy-retreat-plan-commit-suicide-article-1.1284599.

13. Ibid.

14. Karen Brocklebank, Facebook, September 4, 2013, https://www.facebook.com/ LettersForNoah.

15. Ibid., August 26, 2013.

16. Ibid., February 8, 2014.

17. Allana Maiden, in a phone interview with the authors, April 1, 2013.

18. Ibid.

19. Ibid.

20. Nina Strochlic, "'How an Online Campaign May Get Victoria's Secret into 'Survivor Bras,'" *The Daily Beast,* February 1, 2013, http://www.thedailybeast.com /articles/2013/02/01/how-an-online-campaign-may-get-victoria-s-secret-into -survivor-bras.html.

21. Sugata Mitra, "Build a School in the Cloud," TED, February 2013, https:// www.ted.com/talks/sugata_mitra_build_a_school_in_the_cloud.

22. World Population Review, "India Population 2014," March 26, 2014, http:// worldpopulationreview.com/countries/india-population/.

23. Sugata Mitra, "The Child-Driven Education," TED, July 2010, https://www.ted .com/talks/sugata_mitra_the_child_driven_education/transcript?language=en.

24. Mitra, "Build a School in the Cloud."

25. Joshua Davis, "How a Radical New Teaching Method Could Unleash a Generation of Geniuses," *Wired,* October 15, 2013, http://www.wired.com/2013/10 /free-thinkers/all/.

26. *EDU.Blog.com,* "Sugata Mitra: The Granny Cloud," blog entry by Ewan McIntosh, January 19, 2011, http://edu.blogs.com/edublogs/2011/01/sugata -mitra-the-granny-cloud.html.

27. Johns Hopkins Medicine, "Gaining Health while Giving Back to the Community," April 2004, http://www.hopkinsmedicine.org/press_releases/2004/04_06 _04.html.

28. Linnea Covington, "Food Blogger, 9, Crusades For Better School Lunches," *Today,* May 23, 2012, http://www.today.com/food/food-blogger-9-crusades-better -school-lunches-790083.

29. Ravi Somaiya, "Girl 9 Gives School Lunch Failing Grade," *The New York Times,* June 15, 2012, http://www.nytimes.com/2012/06/16/world/europe/girl -9-gives-school-lunch-failing-grade.html.

30. *NeverSeconds Blog,* "Today Was Very Different at Lunchtime," blog entry by Martha Payne, May 2012, http://neverseconds.blogspot.com/2012/05/today -was-very-different-at-lunchtime.html.

31. Brendan Carlin and Malcolm Moore, "Oliver's Campaign Bears Fruit," *The Telegraph,* March 31, 2005, http://www.telegraph.co.uk/news/uknews/1486782 /Olivers-campaign-bears-fruit.html.

32. Alexandra Sifferlin, "9-Year-Old Food Blogger Takes on School Lunch," *Time,* May 25, 2012, http://healthland.time.com/2012/05/25/9-year-old-food-blogger -takes-on-school-lunch/.

33. *NeverSeconds Blog*, "New Things from Yesterday Radishes," blog entry by Martha Payne, May 2012, http://neverseconds.blogspot.com/2012/05/new-things-from-yesterday-radishes-mini.html.

34. Susie Boniface, "Food For Thought: Star Pupil Martha Exposes Shocking State of Her School Dinners—and Teaches Grown-Ups a Lesson," *Mirror*, June 15, 2012, http://www.mirror.co.uk/news/uk-news/never-seconds-blog-martha-exposes-884987.

35. Ibid.

36. Ibid.

37. Martha Payne, "Martha Payne: Diary of a Girl Who Fed the Starving," *The Telegraph*, October 4, 2012, http://www.telegraph.co.uk/news/worldnews/africaandindianocean/malawi/9584222/Martha-Payne-diary-of-a-girl-who-fed-the-starving.html.

38. Valerie Aguilar, "Maria Theresa Kumar," *BellaOnline*, http://www.bellaonline.com/articles/art35108.asp.

39. "Raising Our Voices: Meet Maria Theresa Kumar, Founder of Voto Latino," *Woman's Day*, http://www.womansday.com/life/personal-stories/maria-teresa-kumar.

40. Ibid.

41. Ibid.

CHAPTER 7

1. *The Green Book: A Guide to Members' Allowances* (Westminster: House of Commons, March 2009), 59-60.

2. "MP's lose bid to hide expense claims from journalists," *Press Gazette*, May 16, 2008, http://www.pressgazette.co.uk/node/41186.

3. Iain Watson, "Risks and Gains of Expenses Leak," *BBC*, May 9, 2009, http://news.bbc.co.uk/2/hi/uk_news/politics/8041591.stm.

4. Clogdah Hartley, "Millions See Beckett Heckled," *The Sun*, January 12, 2011, http://www.thesun.co.uk/sol/homepage/news/article2432534.ece.

5. "MP's Expenses: All the Revelations, as a Spreadsheet," *The Guardian*, http://www.theguardian.com/news/datablog/2009/may/13/mps-expenses-houseofcommons.

6. Martin Beckford, "MP's Expenses: Two Lavatory Seats in Two Years for John Prescott," *The Telegraph*, May 2009, http://www.telegraph.co.uk/news/newstopics/mps-expenses/5293199/MPs-expenses-Two-lavatory-seats-in-two-years-for-John-Prescott.html.

7. Rosa Prince, "David Milliband Challenged by Gardener: MP's Expenses," *The Telegraph*, May 2009, http://www.telegraph.co.uk/news/newstopics/mps-expenses/5293729/David-Miliband-challenged-by-gardener-MPs-expenses.html.

8. Martin Beckford, "Immigration Minister Claimed for Women's Clothing and Panty Liners," *The Telegraph*, May 2009, http://www.telegraph.co.uk/news/newstopics/mps-expenses/5298364/Immigration-Minister-claimed-for-womens-clothing-and-panty-liners.html.

9. Rosa Prince, "MP's Expenses: Taxpayer Charged for Michael Ancram's Pool," *The Telegraph*, May 2009, http://www.telegraph.co.uk/news/newstopics/mps-expenses/5309953/MPs-expenses-Taxpayer-charged-for-Michael-Ancrams-pool.html.

10. Allegra Stratton, "Bill Cash Battles for Political Life as Expenses Row Threatens More MPs," *Guardian,* May 2009, http://www.theguardian.com/politics/2009/may/29/bill-cash-conservatives-mps-expenses.

11. Kevin Maguire, "Where Do You Rank in the Official Earnings List? Figures Reveal Huge Pay Gap Between the Rich and Poor," *Mirror,* January 9, 2014, http://www.mirror.co.uk/news/uk-news/uk-average-salary-26500-figures-3002995.

12. Iain Martin, "MPs Expenses: A Scandal That Will Not Die," *The Telegraph,* April 13, 2014, http://www.telegraph.co.uk/news/newstopics/mps-expenses/10761548/MPs-expenses-A-scandal-that-will-not-die.html.

13. Mike Butcher, "Guardian Releases Crowdsourcing App to Pick Over MP's Expenses," *TechCrunch,* June 18, 2009, http://techcrunch.com/2009/06/18/guardian-releases-crowd-sourcing-app-to-pick-over-mps-expenses/.

14. Clive Thompson, *Smarter Than You Think: How Technology Is Changing Our Minds for the Better,* (New York: Penguin Group 2013).

15. Michael Anderson, "Four Crowdsourcing Lessons from the Guardian's Spectacular Expenses Scandal," *Neiman Lab,* June 23, 2009, http://www.niemanlab.org/2009/06/four-crowdsourcing-lessons-from-the-guardians-spectacular-expenses-scandal-experiment/.

16. Ibid.

17. Ibid.

18. TED, "Seth Cooper," http://www.tedmed.com/speakers/show?id=6591.

19. Clive Thompson, "Clive Thompson: Towards the Hive Mind," *National Post,* November 28, 2013, http://fullcomment.nationalpost.com/2013/11/28/clive-thompson-toward-the-hive-mind/.

20. Rachel Botsman, *What's Mine Is Yours: The Rise of Collaborative Consumption,* (New York: HarperCollins, 2010).

21. Ibid.

22. Let's Do It, "Statistics," http://www.letsdoitworld.org/statistics.

23. Let's Do It, "About World Cleanup." http://www.letsdoitworld.org/about.

24. Let's Do It, "Let's Create the Biggest and Ugliest Map Ever," March 23, 2011, http://www.letsdoitworld.org/news/lets-create-biggest-and-ugliest-map-ever.

25. Saul Kaplan, *The Business Model Innovation Factory: How to Stay Relevant When the World Is Changing,* (New York: Wiley, 2012).

26. Small Business Professor, "The Gem Plumbing Dynasty," http://www.smallbusinessprof.com/case-studies/gem-plumbing.php.

27. Scott Sayare, "A Dictator Is Gone, but Egypt's Traffic and Congestion Seem Immovable," *The New York Times,* September 10, 2012, http://www.nytimes.com/2012/09/11/world/middleeast/for-egyptians-no-relief-from-cairos-infamous-traffic.html?pagewanted=all&_r=0.

28. Ibid.

29. Reem Leila, "Beating the Traffic Together," *Al-Ahram Weekly,* May 2, 2014, http://weekly.ahram.org.eg/Print/5314.aspx.

30. Sayare, "A Dictator Is Gone, but Egypt's Traffic and Congestion Seem Immovable."

31. Bey2ollak, "Bey2ollak, 'We Empower People to Fight Traffic Together," http://desktop.bey2ollak.com/about-bey2ollak/.

32. "Co-founder of Bey2ollak: Entrepreneurship is the only solution for developing Egypt," *DailyNews Egypt,* September 1, 2013, http://www.dailynewsegypt

.com/2013/09/01/co-founder-of-bey2ollak-entrepreneurship-is-the-only-solu
tion-for-developing-egypt/.

33. Bey2ollak, "Bey2ollak; 'We Empower People to Fight Traffic Together.'"
34. Reem Leila, "Beating the Traffic Together."
35. Ibid.
36. Nancy Messieh, "Beyollak, an Egyptian Startup Success Story to Aspire To," *The Next Web,* July 17, 2011, http://thenextweb.com/me/2011/07/17/bey2ollak-an
-egyptian-start-up-success-story-to-aspire-to/.
37. Ibid.
38. Soutik Biswas, "Digital Indians: Rikin Gandhi Helps Farmers with Videos," *BBC,* September 11, 2013, http://www.bbc.com/news/technology-23867132.
39. Ian Steadman, "Digital Green Uses Social Networking to Improve Farm-
ing Knowledge," *Wired,* November 14, 2012, http://www.wired.co.uk/news
/archive/2012-11/14/farmerbook.
40. Ibid.
41. Ibid.
42. Ibid.
43. Ibid.
44. Ibid.
45. Luis von Ahn, "Massive Scale Online Collaboration," TED, December 2011, https://www.ted.com/talks/luis_von_ahn_massive_scale_online_collabora
tion/transcript.
46. Ibid.
47. Saj-nicole Joni, "Help Yourself and Help the World: An Interview With Duolingo CEO Luis von Ahn," *Forbes,* May 28, 2014, http://www.forbes.com/sites
/forbesleadershipforum/2014/05/28/help-yourself-and-help-the-world-an-inter
view-with-duolingo-ceo-luis-von-ahn/.
48. Von Ahn. "Massive Scale Online Collaboration."
49. Ibid.
50. Joni, "Help Yourself and Help the World."
51. Ibid.
52. Ibid.
53. Luis von Ahn, "Massive Scale Online Collaboration [video]," TED, December 2011, https://www.ted.com/talks/luis_von_ahn_massive_scale_online_collabo
ration?language=en#t-833641
54. Joni, "Help Yourself and Help the World."
55. Ibid.

CHAPTER 8

1. Simon Hattenstone, "Pharrell Williams: My Music Is so Much Bigger Than Me, and What I Am," *The Guardian,* March 7, 2014, http://www.theguardian.com
/music/2014/mar/08/pharrell-williams-interview-daft-punk.
2. Zach Baron, "How Pharrell Williams on Advanced Style Moves and that Oscar Snub: My Song Will Be Here for 10 Years," *GQ,* March 2014, http://www
.gq.com/entertainment/profiles/201404/pharrell-williams-oscar-snub.
3. Ibid.
4. I am Other, "About," http://iamother.com/about.

5. Brain Athlete, "The Closest Friendships of Albert Einstein," http://brainathlete.com/closest-friendships-albert-einstein/.

6. Kevin Brown, *Reflections on Relativity,* October 2013, http://www.mathpages.com/rr/s3-08/3-08.htm.

7. Joshua Shenk, *Powers of Two: Finding the Essence of Innovation in Creative Pairs* (New York: Houghton Mifflin Harcourt, 2014).

8. Ibid.

9. Ayana Byrd, "How Pharrell's Creative Director Is Making the World Happy," *Fast Company,* July 1, 2014, http://www.fastcompany.com/3032361/innovation-agents/how-pharrells-creative-director-is-making-the-world-happy.

10. Collaborative Fund, "About," http://collaborativefund.com/about/collaborative-fund/.

11. Ibid.

12. Zack Baron, "Pharrell Williams Is Finally Happy," *GQ,* February 27, 2014, http://www.gq.com/entertainment/profiles/201402/pharrell-girl-album-exclusive.

13. Kenji Yoshino, *Covering: The Hidden Assault of Our Civil Rights,* (New York: Random House, 2006).

14. Christie Smith, in a phone interview with the authors, April 20, 2014.

15. Ibid.

16. Powerhouse Museum, "Slim Fit Burqini by Ahiida," 2011, http://www.powerhousemuseum.com/mob/collection/database/?irn=435338.

17. Ibid.

18. Ibid.

19. Ibid.

20. Ibid.

21. Liz Jackson, "Riot and Revenge," Australian Broadcasting Corporation, March 13, 2006, http://www.abc.net.au/4corners/content/2006/s1590953.htm.

22. "Man Charged over Sydney Messages," *BBC,* December 22, 2005, http://news.bbc.co.uk/2/hi/asia-pacific/4551356.stm.

23. Jackson, "Riot and Revenge."

24. Powerhouse Museum, "Slim Fit Burqini by Ahiida."

25. Frans Johansson, *The Medici Effect: What Elephants and Epidemics Can Teach Us About Epidemics* (Boston: Harvard Business Review Press, 2006).

26. Pat Mitchell, in an interview with the authors, March 13, 2014.

27. Ibid.

28. Ibid.

29. Susan Sontag, "Illness as Metaphor," *New York Review of Books,* January 26, 1978, http://www.nybooks.com/articles/archives/1978/jan/26/illness-as-metaphor/.

30. Michelle Dean, "A Note on Nerdfighters," *The New Yorker,* March 13, 2013, http://www.newyorker.com/online/blogs/culture/2013/03/a-note-on-nerdfighters.html.

31. Urban Dictionary.com, "Nerdfighter," http://www.urbandictionary.com/define.php?term=Nerdfighter.

32. Wikihow.com, "How to Be a Nerdfighter," http://www.wikihow.com/Be-a-Nerdfighter.

33. Dean, "A Note on Nerdfighters."

34. Vlog brothers, "Rest in Awesome, Esther," YouTube, August 27, 2010, http://www.youtube.com/watch?v=Mj96HM9kDTQ.

35. Wikihow.com, "How to Be a Nerdfighter."

CHAPTER 9

1. Carl Zimmer, "The Girl Who Turned to Bone," *The Atlantic,* May 22, 2013, http://www.theatlantic.com/magazine/archive/2013/06/the-mystery-of-the-se cond-skeleton/309305/.
2. Ibid.
3. Ibid.
4. Ibid.
5. Ibid.
6. Ibid.
7. Centers for Disease Control and Protection, "Osteoporosis or Low Bone Mass at the Femur Neck or Lumbar Spine in Older Adults," April 2012, http://www.cdc .gov/nchs/data/databriefs/db93.htm.
8. *Knight Blog,* "The Power of Crowd Wisdom in Solving Difficult Medi- cal Cases," blog entry by Thomas Krafft, March 27, 2014, http://www .knightfoundation.org/blogs/knightblog/2014/3/27/power-crowd-wisdom -solving-difficult-medical-cases/.
9. Crowdsourcing.org, "CrowdMed Adds Crowd Wisdom to the Medical Com- munity," April 17, 2013, http://www.crowdsourcing.org/editorial/crowdmed -adds-crowd-wisdom-to-the-medical-community/25332.
10. Liat Clark, "Medical Web Tool Lets the Crowd Diagnose Your Illness," *Wired,* April 17, 2013, http://www.wired.co.uk/news/archive/2013-04/17/crowdmed.
11. Carolyn Johnson, "Thorny Research Problems, Solved by Crowdsourcing," *Boston Globe,* February 11, 2013, http://www.bostonglobe.com/business/2013/02/11 /crowdsourcing-innovation-harvard-study-suggests-prizes-can-spur-scientific -problem-solving/JxDkOkuIKboRjWAoJpM0OK/story.html/.
12. Diabetes Mine, "Harvard Culls New Type I Diabetes Research Ideas," Octo- ber 13, 2010, http://www.diabetesmine.com/2010/10/harvard-culls-new-type-1 -diabetes-research-ideas.html.
13. Eliot van Buskirk, "Harvard-Based Crowdsource Project Seeks New Diabetes Answers—and Questions," *Wired,* February 3, 2010, http://www.wired.com /2010/02/crowdsourcing-rewires-harvard-medical-researchers-brain/.
14. Eva Guinan, Kevin J. Boudreau and Karim R. Lakhani, "Experiments in Open Innovation at Harvard Medical School," *MIT Sloan Management Re- view,* March 19, 2013, http://sloanreview.mit.edu/article/experiments-in-open -innovation-at-harvard-medical-school/.
15. Ibid.
16. The World Bank, "Curbing Air Pollution in Mongolia's Capital," April 25, 2012, http://www.worldbank.org/en/news/feature/2012/04/25/curbing-air-pollution -in-mongolia-capital.
17. Jeffrey Young, "The Student Becomes the Teacher," *Slate,* April 23, 2014, http:// www.slate.com/articles/technology/future_tense/2014/04/battushig_myan ganbayar_aced_an_edx_mooc_then_gave_lessons_to_mit.2.html.
18. Laura Pappano, "The Boy Genius of Ulan Bator," *The New York Times,* Septem- ber 13, 2013, http://www.nytimes.com/2013/09/15/magazine/the-boy-genius -of-ulan-bator.html?pagewanted=all.
19. Young, "The Student Becomes the Teacher."
20. Pappano, "The Boy Genius of Ulan Bator."

21. Elizabeth Hone, "The Gardener Who Nurtured London's Crystal Palace," *Christian Science Monitor,* October 4, 1980, http://www.csmonitor.com/1980/1024/102456.html.
22. Ibid.
23. Herbert George Wells, *The Time Machine* (New York: Signet Classics, 1984), 87.
24. Architects for Peace, "Curriculum Vitae: Mick Pearce," http://www.architectsforpeace.org/mickprofile.php.
25. Janine Benyus, *Biomimicry: Innovation Inspired by Nature* (New York: Harper Perrenial, 2002).
26. Architects for Peace, "Curriculum Vitae: Mick Pearce."
27. Abigal Doan, "Biomimetic Architecture: Green Building in Zimbabwe Modeled after Termite Mounds," *Inhabitat,* November 29, 2012, http://inhabitat.com/building-modelled-on-termites-eastgate-centre-in-zimbabwe/.
28. Ibid.
29. Chris Fischer, in a phone interview with the authors, October 31, 2013.
30. Ibid.
31. *National Wildlife Foundation Blog,* "Is There Still Hope for Sharks?," March 21, 2012, http://blog.nwf.org/2012/03/wildlife-week-is-there-still-hope-for-sharks/.
32. Chris Fischer, in a phone interview with the authors, October 31, 2013.
33. National Geographic Channel, "Chris Fischer," https://natgeotv.com/za/shark-men/biographies.
34. Chris Fischer, in a phone interview with the authors, October 31, 2013.
35. Ibid.
36. Ibid.
37. Ibid.

PULLING IT ALL TOGETHER

1. Gloria Steinem, "Q&A," http://www.gloriasteinem.com/qa/.
2. Andre Gide, *The Counterfeiters* (New York: Vintage Books, 1973), 353.
3. Oscar Wilde, *The Importance of Being Earnest a Trivial Comedy for Serious People by the Author of Lady Windermere's Fan"* (London: Leonard Smithers and Co., 1898.), 15.
4. Seth Godin, *Tribes: We Need You to Lead Us* (New York: Portfolio, 2008), 37.
5. Bombay Sarvoyda Mandal and Gandhi Research Foundation, "The Power of Non-Violence," http://www.mkgandhi.org/nonviolence/phil2.htm.
6. Antoine de Saint-Exupéry, *Flight to Arras* (New York: Harcourt, 1986), 129.
7. Maria Popova, in an interview with the authors, August 31, 2014.
8. Nelson Mandela.org, "Selected Quotes," http://www.nelsonmandela.org/content/mini-site/selected-quotes.
9. Kathy Caprino, "10 Lessons I Learned from Sara Blakely," *Forbes,* May 23, 2012, http://www.forbes.com/sites/kathycaprino/2012/05/23/10-lessons-i-learned-from-sara-blakely-that-you-wont-hear-in-business-school/.
10. Katharine Hepburn and Susan Crimp, *Katharine Hepburn Once Said . . . : Great Lines to Live By* (New York: HarperCollins, 2003), 30.
11. Richard Pascale, Jerry Sternin and Monique Sternin, *The Power of Positive Deviance: How Unlikely Innovators Solve the World's Toughest Problems* (Boston: Harvard Business Press, 2010), 38.

INDEX